COMP
PROGRA
IN B

Lionel Carter is a qualified Chartered Mechanical Engineer. He is Principal Lecturer in Management Science at Slough College of Higher Education and has been a visiting lecturer at Brunel University. Previously he was an operational research consultant in industry.

Dr Eva Huzan is Head of Research and Development in Computing at Slough College of Higher Education. Previously she worked as a physicist and computing lecturer in industry. She has carried out research in computing and physics at the London School of Economics and Political Science, and Queen Mary College, University of London.

TEACH YOURSELF BOOKS

COMPUTER PROGRAMMING IN BASIC

L. R. Carter and E. Huzan

TEACH YOURSELF BOOKS

Hodder and Stoughton

First published 1981
Second edition 1987
Third impression 1991

British Library Cataloguing in Publication Data
Carter, L. R.
Computer programming in BASIC.—2nd ed.
—(Teach yourself books).
1. BASIC (Computer program language)
I. Title   II. Huzan, E.
005.13′3   QA76.73.B3

ISBN 0 340 41765 X

Printed and bound in England
for Hodder and Stoughton Educational,
a division of Hodder and Stoughton Ltd,
Mill Road, Dunton Green, Sevenoaks, Kent
by Clays Ltd, St Ives plc.
Photoset by Rowland Phototypesetting Ltd,
Bury St Edmunds, Suffolk

Contents

List of Figures   vi
List of Tables   vii

Introduction   xi

1.   Introduction to Computers and Programming   1
2.   Simple Input and Output Statements   5
3.   Arithmetic Operations   13
4.   Program Development   21
5.   Conditional and Unconditional Branching   28
6.   Functions   38
7.   Colour and Graphics   53
8.   Arrays   71
9.   Subroutines   79
10.   Sound   90
11.   Range of Applications   96
12.   Using a Printer and Disk Unit   111
13.   Using Data Files   121
14.   File Processing and Reporting Example   128

Appendices
A   Programs   148
B   Answers to Problems   159
C   ASCII Code (64 Character Set)   161

Index   165

List of Figures

Figure 1.1	Basic units of a computer	2
Figure 4.1	Some flowchart symbols	24
Figure 4.2	Flowchart for average of three numbers	25
Figure 4.3	A trace through a program	27
Figure 5.1	Flowchart to illustrate loop control	30
Figure 5.2	Rectangle output from program	37
Figure 6.1	Output from clock program	52
Figure 7.1	'Mirror images' of positions 4,3 in top left-hand quadrant	57
Figure 7.2	Displacement of PAINT coordinate in step with triangle	64
Figure 8.1	Sorting a list of numbers into ascending order	77
Figure 9.1	Sampling flowchart	88
Figure 12.1	Output from printer control program	111
Figure 13.1	General flow with dummy record	126
Figure 14.1	Command menu for stock recording program	129
Figure 14.2	Outline flowchart	131

List of Tables

Table 2.1	Prompts and data for program	9
Table 2.2	Name and address program	10
Table 3.1	Contents of X, Y and S	13
Table 3.2	Program to illustrate order of evaluation	15
Table 3.3	Contents of B, C, D, E and A	16
Table 3.4	LET statements	16
Table 3.5	Data read and final results	17
Table 3.6	Changes to arithmetic expressions	18
Table 3.7	Results of arithmetic operations	18
Table 3.8	Output from 'Number of £s required' program	19
Table 3.9	Output from 'Cost of stationery' program	20
Table 4.1	Program containing an error	26
Table 5.1	Relational operators	30
Table 5.2	Terminating with a dummy value	31
Table 5.3	Program to add N numbers	31
Table 5.4	Program with nested IFs and ELSE	32
Table 5.5	Alternative program to add N numbers	33
Table 5.6	Start, end and step variables	34
Table 5.7	Start, end and step expressions	34
Table 5.8	Calculations for different codes	35
Table 5.9	Program to output a rectangle	36
Table 6.1	Rounding to nearest minute	40
Table 6.2	Use of SGN and SQR	41
Table 6.3	Calculation of diameters of cylindrical tanks	41
Table 6.4	Output from program given in Table 6.3	42
Table 6.5	Program to round numbers	46
Table 6.6	Some solids with uniform cross-sectional areas	47
Table 6.7	Data for 'Volumes of solids' problem	48
Table 6.8	Clock for two players program	50
Table 7.1	Demonstration of foreground, screen and border colours	54

Table 7.2	Coloured mosaic patterns	55
Table 7.3	Palette colours	60
Table 7.4	Program to draw five overlapping triangles	62
Table 7.5	Program to draw overlapping coloured rectangles	64
Table 7.6	Program to draw and paint ellipses	66
Table 7.7	Coloured pie chart example	66
Table 7.8	Program to draw a house	69
Table 8.1	Program to output numbers > 10 and negative numbers	71
Table 8.2	Output from program given in Table 8.1	72
Table 8.3	Input data for 'Nested FOR loops' program	75
Table 8.4	Table to be output	75
Table 8.5	Program using nested FOR loops	75
Table 8.6	Sorting a list of numbers	78
Table 9.1	Serial plotting routine	81
Table 9.2	Pastureland in a parish	81
Table 9.3	Percentage pastureland output	82
Table 9.4	Frequency grouping routine	83
Table 9.5	Frequency table routine	83
Table 9.6	Histogram routine	84
Table 9.7	Parish data	85
Table 9.8	Frequency table for Problem 2	85
Table 9.9	Histogram for Problem 2	86
Table 9.10	Data to be sampled	86
Table 9.11	Contents of $X(R, I)$	87
Table 9.12	Sampling routine	87
Table 10.1	Demonstration of full range of notes	92
Table 10.2	Demonstration of different tempos	92
Table 10.3	Playing a tune	93
Table 10.4	Two-tone siren	94
Table 10.5	Ringing phone program	94
Table 10.6	Demonstration of SOUND statement	95
Table 11.1	Program to calculate e^x	96
Table 11.2	'Heat of combustion' problem	97
Table 11.3	Output from Table 11.2 and data input	98
Table 11.4	Quadratic equations	98
Table 11.5	Tabulation of results for Problem 3	99
Table 11.6	Linear regression routine	101
Table 11.7	Data for Problem 4	103
Table 11.8a	Main routine for simulation program	104
Table 11.8b	Main routine for simulation program (cont.)	105
Table 11.9	Example of output from Table 11.8	106
Table 11.10	Failure pattern of units	107
Table 11.11	Program for mortgage calculation	109

Table 11.12	Example of output from Table 11.11	110
Table 12.1a	Enhanced name and address program	112
Table 12.1b	Enchanced name and address program (cont.)	113
Table 12.2	Demonstration of printer control	115
Table 13.1	Stock records	122
Table 13.2	Output from reorder program	126
Table 13.3	Output from search program	127
Table 14.1	Example of output for search option	132
Table 14.2	Example of output for reorder report	133
Table 14.3	Example of output for valuation report	133
Table 14.4	Initialisation and start-up routine	134
Table 14.5	File load routine	134
Table 14.6	Main program and menu subroutine	136
Table 14.7	Add record routine	137
Table 14.8	Change record routine	139
Table 14.9	Delete record routine	141
Table 14.10	Exit program routine	142
Table 14.11	Reorder report routine	143
Table 14.12	Search records routine	145
Table 14.13	Update stock routine	146
Table 14.14	Valuation report routine	147
Table A1	Number of £s required	148
Table A2	Cost of stationery	148
Table A3	Using the ON . . . GOTO statement	149
Table A4	Centring a rectangle	149
Table A5	Radius of circumcircle	150
Table A6	Volumes of solids	150
Table A7	Copying an array	151
Table A8	Sum of elements	151
Table A9	Sorting a list of numbers	152
Table A10	Plot of percentage pastureland	152
Table A11	Pastureland histogram	152
Table A12	Input subroutine	153
Table A13	Timer alarm	153
Table A14	Cos X	154
Table A15	Roots of quadratic equations	154
Table A16	Width of a slit	155
Table A17	Stock data file creation	156
Table A18	Reorder list	157
Table A19	Stock file search	158

Introduction

This book is designed to enable you to learn to program a computer in easy stages and in a methodical way, using the BASIC programming language. You will find that most computers accept programs written in this language.

A computer, compared with a non-programmable calculator, is able to store in its memory the complete set of instructions needed to solve a particular problem. Available instructions include those to read data, to perform calculations and compare values, and to output results. The computer will work through the programmed instructions automatically once the run has been initiated. Chapter 1 explains how computers perform these functions and the typical equipment that comprises a computer system.

The computer that you may have access to will have a set of system commands which you will need to learn before you can enter BASIC programs into it and run the programs with data. These commands vary according to the system you are using.

You will need to become familiar with the few essential commands required for running BASIC on *your system* when you begin to study the language in Chapter 2. When you have completed Chapter 2, you should be able to write and run some very simple BASIC programs.

Arithmetic operations are covered in Chapter 3, and, as in subsequent chapters, examples are given within the text together with problems for you to program and run on your computer. You can compare your programs with those listed in Appendix A; answers to the problems, where these are not given in the text, will be found in Appendix B.

For problems other than very simple ones you must plan and

design your programs in such a way that you ensure that all requirements are met and the likelihood of errors is minimised. Chapter 4 suggests an approach to help you develop programs efficiently.

Having learnt the essential features of programming, you will need additional BASIC statements to enable you to program 'real' problems. Chapters 5, 6, 8 and 9 deal with branching, functions, arrays and subroutines, respectively. The routines developed may be used in a variety of programs and this is further illustrated in Chapter 11.

BASIC is the acronym for Beginners' All-purpose Symbolic Instruction Code, and was designed and used originally for teaching programming. Since then many extensions have been made to it. In particular, BASIC may now be used for the creation and processing of data files on secondary storage devices, such as disk units, as explained in Chapters 12, 13 and 14.

Colour, graphics and sound facilities are available with many microcomputers and you can incorporate these in your BASIC programs, as explained in Chapters 7 and 10. It is important to note that the BASIC statements used for printing, file processing, colour, sound and graphics are *not standard*. The version of BASIC used in all the programs in this book is Advanced BASIC (BASICA) by Microsoft as commonly used on IBM Personal Computers and compatibles.

The applications dealt with in this book include:

colour, graphics and sound effects;
cost calculations and mortgage calculations;
stock file processing and simulation;
processing scientific and engineering data;
simple and more complex mathematical calculations.

These by no means exhaust the types of applications for which you can use your computer. Once you have mastered these simple applications you will be able to start using your computer for more sophisticated tasks.

1

Introduction to Computers and Programming

1.1 Basic functions and units of a computer

An essential function of a computer is the ability to store the set of instructions required to process a particular task. This set of instructions (the *program*), which is prepared by a programmer, has to be held in the computer's store (its main *memory*) while the instructions are followed.

Each computer has a fixed instruction set which it can execute. A *control unit* selects the instructions, one at a time, from the memory, decodes or interprets them and causes the computer to carry out the instruction. If the instruction requires an arithmetic operation to be performed then the control unit transfers the necessary data between the memory and the *arithmetic and logic unit.*

The main memory, arithmetic and logic unit, and control unit comprise the central part of the computer, and together are known as the *central processor.*

Input and *output* peripheral devices, linked to the central processor, are used to insert programs and data into the computer's memory and to output results from there. The information can be keyed in directly from a keyboard (similar to that of a typewriter). Results may be displayed on a television screen or visual display unit, or, if a 'hard' copy is required, printers are available which print either one character or a complete line at a time across a page. Graph plotters may also be used as output peripherals.

Programs may be stored magnetically on *backing* or *secondary storage* devices, and these can then be read back into the computer's memory when required. Typical secondary storage devices are magnetic disks (both hard and floppy disks) and magnetic tape (reel to reel or cassette).

Secondary storage devices are also used to hold files or data records. These are transferred to and from the computer's memory under program control for file processing applications.

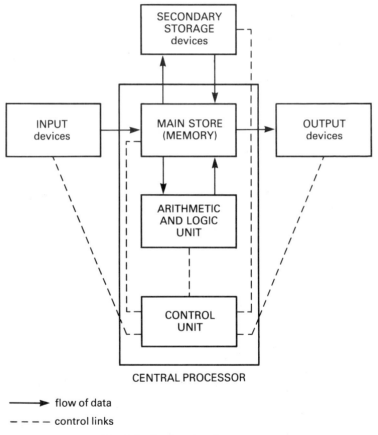

Fig. 1.1   Basic units of a computer

Figure 1.1 shows the basic units of a computer, the flow of data and control links.

1.2 How information is held

A computer is largely made up of a number of two-state devices. The 'off' state of the device may be considered to represent a 0 and the 'on' state a 1. A numbering system comprising only 0s and 1s is called a *binary system*. Different patterns of these binary digits (or *bits*) may be used to represent a character set and ranges of numbers. A group of eight bits is known as a *byte* and can be used to represent a character.

Standard codes have been established by different organisations. The American Standard Code for Information Interchange (ASCII) has been widely adopted, and a table showing the binary representations for a 64 character set is shown in Appendix C (page 161). This is the character set that is most commonly available. Extensions to the ASCII 64 character set allow the representation of additional characters such as lower case alphabet characters (a, b, c etc.).

Numbers are represented in the computer's memory as a combination of bits. The number of bits available to represent a number varies with the computer used. From the BASIC user's point of view, the two factors that should be established are the precision of the decimal number and the range of numbers that can be held in the computer.

1.3 Programming a computer

Each family of processors has its own instruction set which is likely to differ from that of other processors. This means that a particular processor is only capable of understanding its own set of instructions in *binary code*.

The computer's memory can be considered as consisting of a number of cells capable of storing binary patterns representing program instructions or data. Each of these cells is uniquely numbered so that reference can be made to particular memory cells, either to select a program instruction or data, or to write data into a certain memory cell.

High-level languages have been devised which allow several machine code instructions to be expressed in one statement. BASIC is such a programming language, as shown in the example below:

LET C = A + B

is a BASIC statement which causes the two numbers, held in memory cells A and B, to be added together and the sum stored in memory cell C.

However, BASIC programs cannot be understood directly by the computer. BASIC programs need to be translated into machine code using a *compiler* or *interpreter*. The basic difference between these two is the stage at which the translation from BASIC into machine code is performed. Using a compiler, the translation is done *before* the program is executed; this gives speed advantages over an interpreter which performs the translation process as it executes the program. The BASIC interpreter is particularly suitable for first-time users because it has been designed so that programs can easily be altered and corrected.

2

Simple Input and Output Statements

2.1 READ, DATA, INPUT and PRINT statements

This chapter explains how you may enter information into your computer (*input*), and how the computer may be programmed to supply information, for example on a printer or video screen (*output*).

Each BASIC instruction (or statement) consists of a command to the computer to carry out a certain action, and a combination of variables, constants, separators (e.g. a comma) and operators (e.g. +) on which the action is to be performed. For example:

    10 READ A,B,C

tells the computer to read three numbers (numeric constants) from the DATA statement (see line 20 below) and store them in three cells in the computer's memory identified by the names A, B and C. A, B and C are called *variables* and refer to unique numeric addresses, as explained in Chapter 1. When A, B or C are referenced again in the *same* program, the computer will obtain the current contents of these cells. In a *different* program, A, B and C may refer to cells with different actual numeric addresses but unique for *that* program. Single memory cells are referenced in BASIC programs by single letters of the alphabet, A–Z, followed optionally by a single number, 0–9, or another letter A–Z. The actual variable name may be any length in some versions of BASIC but only a certain number of characters may be significant. You need to check this for the system you are using.

The 10 before READ in the statement above is the *line number*. Line numbers enable you to change particular lines in your program by retyping the line. Gaps may be left in the sequence of line numbers for subsequent insertion of additional instructions. Three further instructions complete the program to read and output (PRINT) three numbers:

    20 DATA 25,11,30
    30 PRINT A,B,C
    40 END

The END statement terminates execution of the BASIC program; that is, the processing of the program instructions is stopped.

Note that the following three statements have the same effect as the above READ statement. That is, after these three instructions have been executed with the DATA statement shown in line 20, A, B and C will contain 25, 11 and 30 respectively.

    10 READ A
    11 READ B
    12 READ C

2.2 Entering and editing a program

Type the above small program into your computer exactly as shown, pressing the RETURN key once at the end of each line. After the complete program has been typed in, type LIST and press the RETURN key to check that this has been done correctly.

If there are any mistakes, you can 'edit' the program using your computer's *full screen editor*. There are special cursor control keys on the keyboard which allow you to move the cursor to the left and right and up and down. Once you have reached the position of the mistake on the screen, simply type over the mistake with the correct character.

After the correction has been made, press the RETURN key with the cursor still in position over the line which is being modified. On re-listing the program, the corrected version should appear on the screen.

To help you in editing, there are special insert and delete keys which allow insertion and deletion of characters. You can delete a single line by typing its line number and pressing the RETURN key, or a group of lines by typing the word DELETE and specifying the range of lines to be deleted (e.g. DELETE 100–150).

The LIST command can be used to list a particular line (e.g. LIST 30), or groups of lines (e.g. LIST 200–250), or from the beginning of the program to a line number (e.g. LIST –500), or from a line number to the end of the program (e.g. LIST 200–).

When you have entered your program correctly, type in the command RUN and press the RETURN key to initiate execution of your program.

Note in particular how the contents of A, B and C (i.e. 25, 11 and 30) are output and the number of spaces between the numbers. Change the program so that the PRINT statement is as follows:

    30 PRINT A;B;C

and note the spacing between the numbers when a semi-colon is used to separate the variables in a PRINT statement instead of a comma.

To change the data, you will need to alter the numbers in the DATA statement. Alternatively, you may use an INPUT statement instead of READ and DATA statements. Replace the READ and DATA statements in the program by the following statement:

    10 INPUT A,B,C

(delete line 20 by typing 20 and pressing the RETURN key). When run, the computer will output a question-mark (?) to indicate that data should be input from the keyboard.

A heading may be output at the beginning of the output from the computer by putting it in double quotation marks (including any spaces) in a PRINT statement as in the following example:

    28 PRINT "   A";"   B";"   C"
    30 PRINT A;B;C

(*Note*: In computer codes the *same* character is used for open and closed double quotation marks.)

An alternative method of identifying the three numbers is to output A = followed by the number. Experiment with the following statement to obtain the spacing you require (delete line 28):

    30 PRINT "A =";A;" B =";B;" C =";C

The information in the double quotes is output as given in line 30, while A, B and C which are *not* in quotes refer to memory cells. If A, B and C contain 25, 11 and 30 respectively, line 30 will output:

A = 25   B = 11   C = 30

The TAB function may be used to output information in particular column positions on your video screen as illustrated in the following example:

30 PRINT TAB(5);"A =";A;TAB(15);
"B =";B;TAB(25);"C =";C

This will cause A = to be output in positions 5, 6 and 7, followed by the contents of cell A, then B = in positions 15, 16 and 17, followed by the contents of cell B, then C = in positions 25, 26 and 27, followed by the contents of cell C.

The TAB function will be discussed further in subsequent chapters.

2.3   String variables

For many problems it is necessary to input, store and output variable information which consists of a mixture of letters, numbers and special characters, including spaces. Such a series of symbols is called a *string*. Strings may be stored in *string variables*. String variable names are made up in the same way as numeric variable names but are followed by a dollar sign $ (e.g. A$, B$, C$, . . . , Z$).

The constant information given in double quotes previously is termed *a string constant.*

String variables are essential for reading in and manipulating files of information, particularly for business applications. Just a few examples of the use of string variables are given here to give you some initial practice.

Once a program has been written and proved correct, it may be used over and over again with different data, on different occasions and by different people. It is useful, therefore, to output the date the program has been run, and perhaps by whom. Two string variables may be used to input this information and to cause it to be output.

Change and insert statements in the program to output three numbers as follows:

```
10 INPUT A,B,C,D$,N$
26 PRINT
27 PRINT "DATE "; D$,"      ";N$
28 PRINT
```

When this amended program is run, in reply to ? you will need to input three numbers separated by commas (for A, B and C), followed by the date and your name. For example, input data for the above program could be:

? 25,11,30,27/02/87, J.SMITH

Try running this program with different data, different dates and your name. Notice that the PRINT statements at lines 26 and 28 output blank lines.

2.4 Obtaining the required print layout

It is important to design suitable output so that this can be output in different formats for different purposes. Various ways of using name and address information will be used to illustrate this. The program given in Table 2.2 inputs a title (MR, MRS, MISS, etc.), a name and an address, so that this is stored in memory cells referenced by string variables, and outputs a letter heading, notebook label and envelope labels to the screen.

The five LINE INPUT statements shown in Table 2.2 will enable you to enter five lines of data consisting of *strings* of characters which may include spaces and commas (note: when using INPUT, commas are *not* allowed within a string as a comma is used to separate the different items of data). The LINE INPUT statements (lines 20 to 60) contain a 'message' to prompt the user to enter the

Table 2.1   Prompts and data for program

```
TITLE             :Mr
NAME              :J.Smith
1ST  ADDRESS LINE :30, The Avenue
2ND ADDRESS LINE :Kensington
3RD ADDRESS LINE :London, W8
```

correct data (see Table 2.1). No question mark (?) is output when using LINE INPUT instead of INPUT.

Before entering the program, type NEW and press the RETURN key to clear the current program from the computer's memory. If NEW is not used, then lines in the previous program will appear in the one you are typing in, unless the *same* line numbers have been used and are therefore overwritten.

After clearing the current program from memory as described above, type in AUTO 10,10 and press the RETURN key so that line numbers will appear automatically on the screen, starting at line 10. Complete line 10 and press the RETURN key and 20 will then appear on the screen ready for you to complete that line. To exit from AUTO press the CONTROL key and the BREAK key together. You can use AUTO to start at any line number with any increments – for example, AUTO 60,5 would output 60 as the first line number, 65 as the second, etc. (5 being the increment in this case).

The REM (remarks) statements at lines 80, 130 and 210 in Table

Table 2.2 Name and address program

```
10 CLS:PRINT
20 LINE INPUT "TITLE             : ";T$:PRINT
30 LINE INPUT "NAME             : ";N$:PRINT
40 LINE INPUT "1ST ADDRESS LINE : ";A$:PRINT
50 LINE INPUT "2ND ADDRESS LINE : ";B$:PRINT
60 LINE INPUT "3RD ADDRESS LINE : ";C$:PRINT
70 CLS
80 REM LETTER HEADING
90 PRINT TAB(59);A$
100 PRINT TAB(59);B$
110 PRINT TAB(59);C$
120 PRINT:PRINT:PRINT:END
130 REM NOTEBOOK LABEL
140 PRINT:PRINT
150 PRINT TAB(7);"***********************"
160 PRINT:PRINT
170 PRINT TAB(9);N$
180 PRINT:PRINT
190 PRINT TAB(7);"***********************"
200 PRINT:PRINT:PRINT:END
210 REM ENVELOPE LABELS
220 PRINT:PRINT:PRINT
230 PRINT T$;" ";N$;TAB(19);T$;" ";N$
240 PRINT A$;TAB(19);A$
250 PRINT B$;TAB(19);B$
260 PRINT C$;TAB(19);C$
```

2.2 are only listed with the program to explain the program's actions. Note that you can put more than one statement separated by a colon (:) against one line number (as shown in line 10). This avoids using extra line numbers and is shown in several examples in this book. Line 10 has the effect of clearing the screen (CLS) so that the cursor starts in the home position (top left-hand corner of the screen) when the first PRINT instruction is executed. This means that the first LINE INPUT message will be displayed on the second row on the screen when the program is RUN.

When the END instruction is reached at line 120, execution of the program is stopped but you can continue the processing by typing the command CONT (and pressing the RETURN key). Similarly, use CONT to continue after the Notebook label has been displayed to display the Envelope labels. Execution of the program will terminate after the last line in the program (line 260) has been executed.

The notebook label will contain just the name of the owner in between two lines of asterisks. However, at this stage you will not be able to centralise the name, according to its length, for names of varying length. This will be dealt with in Chapter 12, which contains an enhanced version of the program that outputs letter headings, notebook labels and envelope labels to a printer.

A simple way of outputting to a printer is to use LPRINT instead of PRINT in a program, but Chapter 12 explains a more flexible way of changing from outputting to the screen to outputting to a printer *without* changing PRINT commands. You can output program listings to a printer by using LLIST instead of LIST.

2.5 Saving and loading programs using disks

To save a program on disk, first put your floppy disk in the appropriate drive. Then type SAVE "A:T2–2" and press the RETURN key. A: indicates the drive letter, so if you are saving a program on a different drive type its letter followed by a colon (:) before the file name (in this case T2–2). 'Ok' will appear on the screen when the program has been saved.

To load the saved program into your computer's memory, type LOAD "A:T2–2" when your disk is in drive A, and press the RETURN key.

2.6   Using and defining function keys

Your computer has 10 function keys which are designated F0 to F9. The settings of the function keys are shown on the bottom of the screen. You can turn this display off or on by the commands KEY OFF or KEY ON (remember to press the RETURN key after typing a command to execute it).

F1 to F10 have functions assigned to them when the computer is switched on. You can see the full list of ten functions set by using the command KEY LIST. To change a function, you need to specify the number of the function key and assign a string to it. For example:

    KEY 9,"RENUM"

will assign the renumber function (RENUM) to F9.

RENUM is useful for renumbering program lines to give equal spacing between line numbers after you have inserted or deleted lines in a program. For example, you may want to insert another address line in the program shown in Table 2.2. This will require extra statements, say at lines 65, 115 and 265. RENUM 10,10,10 will give you line numbers which are equally spaced again, each line number being 10 more than the previous one. In this case, the program works equally well if you renumber it or not.

However, if you wanted to insert a sequence of more than nine lines between, say, 120 and 130, then you would need to 'open out' the line numbers. You could start to insert new lines, starting at line 121, between lines 120 and 130 and then renumber from line 121 by

    RENUM 130,121,10

This would renumber the program starting at line 121, which would be changed to 130, and the following line numbers would be equally spaced every 10 again (or 5 or 15 depending on the third number in the RENUM command).

If you have assigned a key as RENUM, just pressing this would give you RENUM 10,10,10, by default, or you can change the values by typing 130,121,10 or whatever is required. Other useful functions to select by using function keys include AUTO, LIST, RUN, CONT, SAVE, LOAD.

3

Arithmetic Operations

3.1 Constants and variables

Your computer may be programmed to perform a variety of calculations by means of arithmetic assignment statements in which the result of the calculation is assigned to a memory cell. For example:

50 LET S = X + Y

causes your computer to add the contents of memory cell X to that of memory cell Y and puts the result in a memory cell called S. X and Y will have had values assigned to them previously, either by an INPUT or READ + DATA statements or by another LET statement. The contents of cells X and Y are unchanged by the action of the LET statement. For example, Table 3.1 shows the contents of X, Y and S before and after execution of the above LET statement, in a program which contains the following statements in addition to line 50 above:

30 READ X, Y
40 DATA 123,56

Note the original, unknown, content of S has been overwritten by the new value 179, the sum of 123 and 56.

Table 3.1   Contents of X, Y and S

Cell	Before	After
X	123	123
Y	56	56
S	?	179

The variables on the right-hand side of the equals sign in a LET statement may be operated on by a number of different arithmetic operators, and may be mixed with constant values (constants). For example:

    51 LET I = I − 1

subtracts 1 from the current value of I, so that after the LET statement has been obeyed I has a value of one less than its previous value. Note that the word LET may be omitted.

The *numeric constants* that may be used are:

(*a*)   whole numbers (*integers*) which do not contain a decimal point, for example, −45,360 (or +360);

(*b*)   numbers containing a decimal point, for example, 8.123, −97.5;

(*c*)   numbers in exponential format, for example, 12.3E4, which represents $12.3 \times 10^4 = 123000$ (4 is called the exponent). The exponent may also be negative, for example, 12.3E − 4, which is $12.3 \times 10^{-4} = 0.00123$.

Note that numbers are made *negative* by putting a minus sign (−) in front of them. A plus sign (+), or *no* sign, indicates the number is *positive*.

Generally, numeric variables are held as double precision numbers unless specified otherwise, that is, they are stored with more digits than single precision numbers. The actual number of digits of precision will depend on the version of BASIC you are using and on your computer.

In the version of BASIC used for the examples in this book, exponential numbers specified with an E are single precision and double precision if D is used instead of E. Integer variables (indicated by a % sign after the variable name) take up least storage and double precision numbers take up most storage. Single precision numbers are shown with a ! sign after the variable name.

For simplicity, numeric constants (non-exponential) and variables are shown in most cases in this book without a type declaration and therefore have the default-type double precision.

Single precision and integer types need only be specified when you need to conserve memory or improve speed of execution. Programs are therefore normally written without specifying a type which results in double precision by default for non-exponential numeric constants and variables.

3.2 Arithmetic operators

The symbols on the right-hand side of the equals sign in a LET statement may consist of variable names, constants and arithmetic operators; this combination of symbols is called an *arithmetic expression*. The *arithmetic operators* indicate which arithmetic operation is to be carried out on the numbers in the arithmetic expression. The following list shows the order in which operations are performed unless changed by the use of brackets as explained in the next section.

Arithmetic operators	Meaning
^	raised to a power (exponentiation)
*,/	multiply, divide
+,−	add, subtract

3.3 Hierarchy of operations

It is possible to use brackets in an arithmetic expression to give the correct meaning. The contents of the brackets are evaluated first starting with the innermost pair of brackets and working outwards. For example, to evaluate

$$\frac{5+9}{4+3}$$

the top line (*numerator*) needs to be added first, then the bottom line (*denominator*) needs to be added, and finally the numerator is divided by the denominator. Brackets are used to ensure this order of evaluation.

A program to illustrate the order of evaluation is given in Table

Table 3.2 Program to illustrate order of evaluation

```
30 READ B,C,D,E
40 DATA 5,9,4,3
50 LET A=(B+C)/(D+E)
70 PRINT B;C;D;E;A
```

3.2; the larger gap in the sequence of line numbers between LET and PRINT statements will allow the insertion of additional statements later. Table 3.3 shows the contents of the memory cells before and after the LET statement in line 50 has been obeyed.

Table 3.3 Contents of B, C, D, E and A

Cell	B	C	D	E	A
Before	5	9	4	3	?
After	5	9	4	3	2

Run this program on your computer and then amend the LET statement as follows (i.e. remove the brackets):

50 LET A = B + C/D + E

A will now be 10.25 (i.e. 9/4 + 5 + 3). This is because the computer evaluates the arithmetic expression in a certain order if there are no brackets, depending on the arithmetic operators in the expression.

If there are no brackets, then the computer will perform the exponentiations first (if there are any), followed by multiplication and division of equal hierarchy, but in the order left to right, lastly addition and subtraction of equal hierarchy. Within brackets the same order of evaluation is carried out, innermost brackets being calculated first as previously stated.

Looking again at the last statement at line 50, you will see that the division C/D, has been carried out first as it is of higher hierarchy than addition. This gives a completely different result from that calculated in the previous LET statement in Table 3.2 where brackets were used.

3.4 Arithmetic expressions and statements

Table 3.4 LET statements

```
30 READ B,C,D,E
40 DATA 5,9,4,3
50 LET A=(B+C)/(D+E)
51 LET G=C/E-B*D
52 LET H=C/(E-B)*D
53 LET J=G-H/E+E^2
61 LET S=C*D-B^A
```

```
62 LET T=(C*D-B)^A
63 LET U=(E*(C-B)^(D/A))
70 PRINT
71 PRINT
72 PRINT "B =";B;" C =";C;" D =";D;" E =";E
73 PRINT
74 PRINT
75 PRINT "A =";A;" G =";G;" H =";H;" J =";J
76 PRINT
77 PRINT
78 PRINT "S =";S;" T =";T;" U =";U
```

Insert all the LET and PRINT statements shown in Table 3.4 into
your program and run it. Output all the results (A,G,H,J,S,T,U)
together with the variable names as identification. The data read
and the final results are shown in Table 3.5.

Table 3.5   Data read and final results

$$B = 5 \quad C = 9 \quad D = 4 \quad E = 3$$
$$A = 2 \quad G = -17 \quad H = -18 \quad J = -2$$
$$S = 11 \quad T = 961 \quad U = 48$$

Notes
1   Line 51 could be replaced by

   51 LET $G = (C/E) - (B*D)$

   to give the same result, although the brackets are unnecessary in
   this case.
2   The brackets in line 52 are essential to give the correct answer, as
   can be seen by comparing the results of line 52 with that of line
   51.
3   In line 53, H is used in the expression because a value was
   assigned to it in line 52. Instead of E^2, you can use $E*E$, which
   is a quicker operation. Amend line 53 to

   53 LET $J = G - H/E + E*E$

   and check that you get the same result for J.
4   In line 61, B^A (i.e. 5^2) is evaluated first, then $C*D$ (i.e. 9×4)
   before the subtraction (i.e. 36−25) is carried out. However, in
   line 62 the contents of the brackets are evaluated first (i.e. 31)
   before this is squared by A.

5 There are three pairs of brackets in line 63. The innermost pair is evaluated first from the left, that is, C − B (equals 4), then D/A is evaluated (equals 2). The exponentiation is carried out next to give 4^2, and finally this is multiplied by E (i.e. 3).

Table 3.6 Changes to arithmetic expressions

```
50 LET A!=(B+C)/(D+E)
51 LET G!=C/(E-B)*D
52 LET H!=C/(E-B*D)
53 LET J!=((G!-H!)/E+E)^2
61 LET S!=C*(D-B)^A!
62 LET T!=C*(D-(B^A!))
63 LET U!=E*C-B^D/A!
```

As a further exercise, change the arithmetic expression in lines 50 to 63 in Table 3.4 to those given in Table 3.6. Check your results with those given in Table 3.7. If your computer has the facility for changing individual characters in a line, use this facility instead of typing whole lines again. Note that some of the variables have been declared single precision by the use of !.

Table 3.7 Results of arithmetic operations

B = 5   C = 9   D = 4   E = 3
A = 2   G = −18   H = −.5294118   J = 7.97232
S = 9   T = −189   U = −285.5

3.5 Problems

You are now ready to attempt some simple problems. For more complicated problems, it is advisable to express the logic in the form of a *flowchart* before coding it in BASIC, as explained in Chapter 4.

In your programs, use constants instead of variables for values that are not going to change during the execution of the program or from one run of the program to the next. Variable names should be meaningful: for example, use E for Expenses.

Write programs and run them on your computer for each of the following problems. If you get errors, reading Chapter 4 will help you to correct them. Compare your programs with those given in Tables A1 and A2 in Appendix A (page 148); substituting actual values in place of the variables will help you understand the action of each instruction. The results from each program for the data given are shown in Tables 3.8 and 3.9. You should experiment with a variety of PRINT statements to give different outputs (e.g. underline answer with hyphens or asterisks, line up values).

Problem 1 – Number of £s required
On your proposed visit to the USA, you will need 150 dollars a night for accommodation and 125 dollars a day for food, travelling and incidental expenses. You intend to stay five nights and wish to take sufficient dollars to have 100 dollars to buy presents. How many pounds sterling will you need to exchange if the exchange rate is 1.5 dollars to the £? (Your program should be flexible enough to cope with changes in expenses, the length of stay and the exchange rate for subsequent visits.)

Table 3.8   Output from 'Number of £s required' program

LENGTH OF STAY (NIGHTS)	: 5
ACCOMMODATION (PER NIGHT)	$: 150
EXPENSES (MEALS ETC.)	$: 125
ALLOWANCE FOR PRESENTS	$: 100
EXCHANGE RATE ($ TO THE £)	: 1.5
POUNDS STERLING REQUIRED	: 983.33

****

Note: For problem 1 you need to specify the POUNDS STERLING REQUIRED to two decimal places. You can do this by using a PRINT USING command. For example, if T holds the number of £s required, then the following two statements will give you the required output:

```
100 PRINT "POUNDS STERLING REQUIRED:";
110 PRINT USING "###.##";T
```

The semi-colon (;) at the end of line 100 causes the output from the next PRINT statement (in line 110) to be displayed on the same line as that from line 100. The #s in line 110 indicate the number of places before and after the decimal point (i.e. the format) for the display of the value held in the variable T. You can output to a printer using LPRINT and LPRINT USING instead of PRINT and PRINT USING. If you are using a matrix printer, it may need setting to produce a £ sign, as explained in Chapter 12, or leave a space for a £ sign to be written in on the printed output.

Problem 2 – Cost of stationery

Calculate the cost of stationery for a course that is being run, given the following information:

Number of delegates attending	58
Cost of folders	14p each
Cost of paper	26p per pad
Cost of pens	12p each

Allow two pens per delegate (there is a quantity discount of 8% for orders over 100 pens). Write the program so that it may also be used on other occasions, when different numbers of delegates will be attending, and allow for changes in costs.

Table 3.9   Output from 'Cost of stationery' program

```
NO OF DELEGATES      : 58
COST OF FOLDERS      : 14 P EACH
COST OF PAPER        : 26 P PER PAD
COST OF PENS LESS 8% : 12 P EACH

TOTAL COST OF STATIONERY = £36.01
****************************************
```

4

Program Development

4.1 The need for pre-planning

This chapter gives you guidance on developing a proposed program. If a program is written too hastily, valuable time may be lost subsequently in implementing the necessary changes. Time spent pre-planning is seldom wasted. Commercial systems designers and programmers are expected to conform to a specific formal procedure. In developing your own programs, you need to exercise self-discipline.

4.2 Understanding the problem

The first step is to ensure that you understand what you intend or are required to do. Are the terms of reference clear? This might mean that you need to check the meaning of any terminology or jargon used. You may also need to ensure you understand the mathematical notation used to specify any relationships involved. Thus, initially, some research or background reading may be necessary. Research may also be necessary when you know what you want to do, but are not sure of the method to be used.

4.3 Designing output

The starting point of designing a program should be the output. You need to consider and make decisions on the following aspects.

The output from a program may be printed and/or written to a file. Is your output going to be solely printed, written to a file or a mixture of both? This leads on to deciding precisely what is to be printed and what is to be written to the file.

For example, your intention may be to write a program to read a stock data file and produce a list of items to reorder. Given, for the moment, that a program can be written to identify the items to be reordered, you need to consider: should the output be solely a printed list or should a reorder file be produced that can be the input to a purchase order program? If you are going to have a printed list of items to be reordered, what should it contain? Should it list the complete stock record of each item or, the other extreme, should it just be a list of stock code numbers?

A program of this nature is developed in Chapter 13; in that case the reorder list consists of stock code, stock description and order quantity. It was not necessary to output the whole record.

Having decided what is to be output, it is then necessary to consider the format and general layout. The considerations to be made are:

In which columns are the variables to be printed?
Should they be truncated or rounded?
Are column headings necessary?
Are main headings necessary?
What spacing is required between headings?
Should headings be underlined?

4.4   Input requirements

Once the output details have been decided you can then identify the necessary input. If a large amount of data is to be processed it may be advisable to read it from a data file; this is dealt with further in Chapter 13. If the data is solely associated with the one program it can be incorporated in DATA statements, while data that varies from run to run is best entered via INPUT statements.

You may not be the only person using the program and this is a factor to be considered. Values should be entered in their most usual form (i.e. 12.5 not .125 for interest rates – see, for example, the mortgage problem in Chapter 11). Ample print messages should be provided, giving guidance, if necessary, as to the input required.

A further aspect of the input design is the desirability of providing some form of control over the program during run time. For example, in the 'Heat of combustion' problem (Chapter 11), the user is asked whether any more data is to be processed and replies Y or N, i.e.

100 INPUT"ANY MORE DATA (Y = YES, N = NO)"; Y$

4.5 Flowcharting

Once you have a broad idea of your requirements the logical sequence of the program statements needs to be developed. This can be done by drawing a flowchart. The more common symbols used in flowcharts are shown in Figure 4.1.

An example of the use of the flowchart symbols is given in Figure 4.2, where it is required to calculate the average of three numbers. The purpose of a flowchart is to ensure the logic is correct before becoming involved with the detail of individual program statements. Further examples of flowcharts will be found elsewhere in this book accompanying the descriptions of programs.

On occasions it becomes apparent from the flowchart or analysis of the problem that a similar calculation will be repeated several times in the program. When a similar set of program statements is likely to be required in several parts of the program, this may indicate the possibility of writing them once only as a *subroutine* and using this routine several times over. A discussion of subroutines is the subject of Chapter 9.

Having drawn flowcharts, the next stage is writing the program. When the program has been written, you still have not finished. A very important part of producing useful programs is to ensure that they perform as intended, and the next section discusses the testing and documentation of your programs.

4.6 Program testing

If you make a mistake in the use of the BASIC language, your computer will detect this and output a message to tell you that there is a *syntax error* in your program. Examples of typical syntax errors are: mistakes in spelling (e.g. IPUT instead of INPUT), wrong instruction formats (e.g. LET X + Y = S instead of LET S =

Symbol   Use

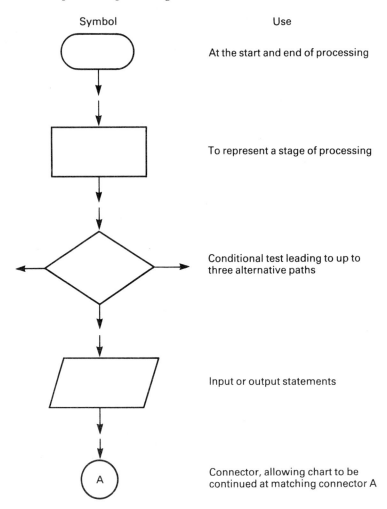

At the start and end of processing

To represent a stage of processing

Conditional test leading to up to
three alternative paths

Input or output statements

Connector, allowing chart to be
continued at matching connector A

Fig. 4.1   Some flowchart symbols

X + Y), and unacceptable variable names (e.g. 2A instead of A2).
You must clear all the syntax errors before you proceed.

Your program may still be incorrect after the syntax errors have
been cleared. You may get an *execution error* caused by asking your
computer to perform an action which it cannot do. For example, if

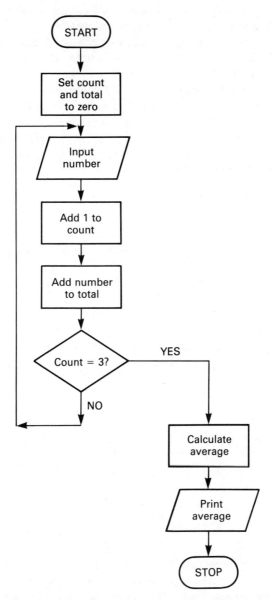

Fig. 4.2 Flowchart for average of three numbers

values are calculated by your program which are either too small or too large you will get arithmetic overflow (this will happen when dividing by zero). An execution error will occur also if you try to assign a string to a numeric variable (e.g. using D instead of D$ for a date, 27/02/87).

A program which runs successfully, without an execution error occurring, may still give the wrong results because the logic of the program is incorrect. You should work through your flowchart and/or program instructions with typical data before running the program on your computer (this is known as performing a dry-run). Then run the program on your computer with this typical data; this should be designed to test every instruction path in the program (i.e. every branch in your flowchart).

Some programming mistakes may still slip through even if you carry out a dry-run, particularly if the program's logic is complicated. You may find the 'bugs' in your program by initiating a trace through it during execution. The TRON command (entered before RUN) causes each line number in the program to be displayed as it is executed. The line numbers are shown in square brackets and will indicate the instruction path followed by the program. The trace is turned off by the TROFF command or when NEW is used. For extensive debugging, you can include TRON and TROFF as statements in your program, and remove these once the program has been debugged.

Table 4.1   Program containing an error

```
10 C=0:T=0
20 INPUT "NUMBER";N
30 C=C+1
40 T=T+N
50 IF C <> 1 THEN 20
60 AV=T/C
70 PRINT "AVERAGE OF";C"NUMBERS =";AV
80 PRINT "************************"
```

Figure 4.3 shows a trace through the program given in Table 4.1, in which the test in line 50 has been mistyped so that the program calculates the average after only one number has been added to the count. This is shown in the trace. The program can be corrected by changing the 1 in line 50 to a 3.

[10][20] NUMBER? 2
[30][40][50][60][70] AVERAGE OF 1 NUMBERS = 2
[80] *************************

Fig. 4.3 A trace through a program

4.7 FRE and CLEAR

During program development you can monitor the amount of
unused memory by using the command FRE(0). Any character can
be used within the brackets; it has no effect on the value returned. In
addition, the smaller amount of memory remaining for the storage
of string variables can be found by using a particular case of FRE,
namely FRE(" "). In practice, if the string space is used up during
execution of the program the error message "Out of string space in
line . . ." is displayed. Both versions of FRE may be used in direct
mode (preceded by PRINT) or within a program.

The value of variables and strings in memory can be set to zero
and null respectively by the use of CLEAR. This command may
also be used within a program to avoid having to clear variables
individually.

4.8 Documentation

It is important to write down details of the program and its use, for
subsequent reference. You will find it useful to include the following
sections in your documentation: Identification, Contents Page,
Summary, Description of the Problem, Specification of the Problem, Input and Output Formats, Use of Program, Interpretation of
Outputs, Modifications, Appendices.

5

Conditional and Unconditional Branching

5.1 Controlling the order in which instructions are obeyed

For most problems your computer needs to be programmed to *repeat* a set of instructions and to execute different sets of instructions in the program according to the requirements for that particular run. This is done by means of *branch* (jump) instructions.

The GOTO instruction causes control to pass to the line number in the statement. That is, the computer will execute next the statement it has branched to and continue to execute the instructions following in sequence until it encounters another branch instruction. For example:

```
50 I = 1
60 PRINT I
70 I = I + 2
80 GOTO 60
```

will cause the odd numbers 1, 3, 5 etc. to be printed. When the computer executes the instruction at line 80, it will always branch to line 60 and obey that instruction followed by line 70. Therefore, the GOTO statement is an unconditional branch instruction, since it is always executed independently of any condition that exists.

However, you will notice that in the above section of a program, there is no instruction which stops the program being executed; it will go on for ever!

To stop the computer executing this set of instructions, you will need to insert a conditional branch instruction. This will perform a

test to see if a condition exists and pass control to a different part of
the program according to the result of the test.

A conditional branch instruction that you may use in BASIC is
the IF . . . THEN statement. For example, to stop the program
which prints odd numbers, you could add the following statement to
those given above:

65 IF I = 21 THEN END

Try running the program and see if it stops after 21 has been printed.
If you replace 21 by an even number, say, 20 or 22, the program will
not stop since I never has this value.

5.2 Loops and their control

This small program that you have just tested has a set of instructions, lines 60 to 80, which are performed repeatedly, thus forming a
loop. The flowchart for this program shows the loop and the branch
out of the loop more clearly (see Figure 5.1). Notice the GOTO 60
instruction is represented by an arrow from box 70 to box 60.

There are several alternative ways of exiting from a loop and for
branching to different parts of a program. The format of the IF . . .
THEN statement is:

line number IF *relational expression* THEN *statement(s)* or *line number*
[ELSE *statement(s)* or *line number*]

The relational expression is the test that is to be performed. If this
test is true (that is, the condition exists), then control passes to the
statement(s) or line number following the THEN. If the test is false,
then control passes to the statement(s) or line number following the
ELSE. If there is no ELSE then control passes to the next line in
sequence.

The relational expression compares two expressions, so that its
format is:

expression relational operator *expression*

You have already used one relational operator in the previous
example = (equal to). The full list is given in Table 5.1.

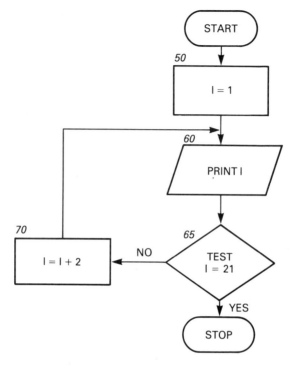

Fig. 5.1 Flowchart to illustrate loop control

Table 5.1 Relational operators

relational operator	meaning
=	equal to
>	greater than
<	less than
>=	greater than or equal to
<=	less than or equal to
<>	not equal to

The IF . . . THEN statement is useful for terminating the inputting of data, as it can be used to test for a final dummy value. This is a value which indicates the end of the data list, but which is not used in the calculations in the program. This is illustrated in Table 5.2, which shows a program to add numbers. The numbers are entered one at a time in response to the INPUT statement in line 40.

Table 5.2 Terminating with a dummy value

```
10 PRINT "ADD NUMBERS"
20 PRINT
30 T=0
40 INPUT X
50 IF X<=0 THEN 80
60 T=T+X
70 GOTO 40
80 PRINT "TOTAL =";T
```

The program in Table 5.2 will stop when either a zero or a negative value is read into X. The IF . . . THEN statement must appear before the calculations involving X, so that the dummy value is not used in the calculations.

Another way to stop repetition of a set of instructions is to specify the number of times the loop has to be carried out, as shown in Table 5.3.

Table 5.3 Program to add N numbers

```
10 INPUT N
20 PRINT "ADD";N;"NUMBERS"
30 PRINT
40 I=0
50 T=0
60 INPUT X
70 T=T+X
80 I=I+1
90 IF I<N THEN 60
100 PRINT "TOTAL =";T
```

If line 40 in Table 5.3 read:

40 I = 1

then line 90 would need to be:

90 IF I < = N THEN 60

This is because the value of I, after line 80 has been obeyed, is one greater than the number of numbers when the loop has been executed N times, if I is set to 1 to start with. This means the loop is terminated when I = N + 1.

5.3   Nested IFs and ELSE

Table 5.4   Program with nested IFs and ELSE

```
10 INPUT "A,B";A,B
20 IF A<>B THEN IF A<B THEN PRINT "A IS LESS THAN B"
                  ELSE PRINT "B IS LESS THAN A"
   ELSE PRINT "A = B"
```

Table 5.4 shows one IF statement inside another one. The *first* ELSE belongs to the *second* IF statement; that is, if A < B is not true, 'B IS LESS THAN A' will be displayed. You can see the result by running the program with suitable data.

Note that the indentations for the nested IFs are obtained by inserting the appropriate number of spaces for the screen width used. When listing on a printer, allow for 80 column lines when calculating the required spacing to give the appropriate indentations.

5.4   Comparing character strings

The IF . . . THEN statement may also be used to compare character strings, since each character is represented by a unique combination of binary digits when stored in the computer. For example, if P$ contains the character H, then:

25 IF P$ = "H" THEN 30

will be true and a branch will be made to line 30.

This facility is particularly useful for comparing names, addresses and similar information for business applications. You will need to refer to a list of codes used to represent characters in your computer's memory to find out which characters have a lower or higher value for greater than or less than tests (see Appendix C (page 161)).

5.5   The FOR . . . NEXT statements

In section 5.2, the number of times a loop was executed was programmed by setting an initial value for the loop counter, testing for a final value, and incrementing the current value of the loop counter if the final value had not been reached. The FOR . . .

NEXT statements have been designed to program these three operations in an easier way.

In the example to add N numbers, in Table 5.3, the variable I (used as the loop counter) was set to an initial value 0. 1 was added to I after the number had been read and added in, and finally a test was carried out $(I < N)$ to determine whether the program should loop back or stop. FOR . . . NEXT statements will be used in an alternative version of the program. The FOR . . . NEXT statements consist of two lines of code. At the beginning of the loop the FOR statement is used to set up the initial conditions, the increment or STEP to be made at the end of the loop and the final value as follows:

line number FOR *variable* = *expression 1* TO *expression 2*
STEP *expression 3*

where expression 1 sets the initial value of the loop counter (also known as the index), expression 2 sets the final value of the loop counter, and expression 3 gives the increment to be added to the variable at the end of each pass through the set of instructions in the loop. If the STEP is equal to 1, both the word STEP and expression 3 may be omitted.

The final instruction in the loop has the format:

line number NEXT *variable*

where the variable has the same name as that given in the associated FOR statement.

The program in Table 5.3 can be amended as shown in Table 5.5. A number will be read into X N times as controlled by the FOR . . . NEXT statements. I is set to 1 initially in line 50, then in line 80 I is incremented by 1 and if it is greater than N the program will go to line 90 and print the total, otherwise it goes back to line 60.

Table 5.5 Alternative program to add N numbers

```
10 INPUT "ENTER VALUE FOR N";N
20 PRINT "ADD";N;"NUMBERS"
30 PRINT
40 T=0
50 FOR I=1 TO N
60     INPUT "ENTER VALUE FOR X";X
70     T=T+X
80 NEXT I
90 PRINT "TOTAL =";T
```

Insert the instruction:

85 PRINT I

so that you can see the value of I after the loop has been executed for the required number of times.

You may use I within the loop, but you should avoid changing I (that is, assigning a new value to I) within the loop as this changes the conditions set up by the FOR . . . NEXT statements. The problem flowcharted in Figure 5.1 may be coded as follows:

50 FOR I = 1 TO 21 STEP 2
60 PRINT I
70 NEXT I

The value of the increment given in the expression following STEP may be negative (so that the loop counter is decremented) or fractional. Table 5.6 shows a program where you can input the start, end and step as variables (A, B and C). Try a number of different combinations, including negative and fractional values, and see what happens. Table 5.7 shows a similar program where expressions have been used in place of simple variables.

Table 5.6   Start, end and step variables

```
10 PRINT "START,END AND STEP VARIABLES"
20 INPUT A,B,C
30 FOR I=A TO B STEP C
40    PRINT I
50 NEXT I
```

Table 5.7   Start, end and step expressions

```
10 PRINT "START,END AND STEP EXPRESSIONS"
20 INPUT A,B,C
30 FOR I=A+1 TO B/2 STEP C-3
40    PRINT I
50 NEXT I
```

5.6   The ON . . . GOTO statement

The format of the ON . . . GOTO statement is

> *line number* ON *expression* GOTO *two or*
> *more line numbers separated by commas*

The integer part of the evaluated expression must be a positive number not greater than the *number* of line numbers after the GOTO part of the statement.

Control will pass to the first, second, third, etc., line number after the GOTO if the integer part of the expression is equal to 1,2,3, etc.

For example, different calculations may need to be carried out according to a code, as in the following problem. A number of sets of data are to be input. Each set consists of a code (1, 2, 3, 4 or 5) and values of X and Y. Calculations are to be performed on each set of data according to the rules shown in Table 5.8.

Table 5.8 Calculations for different codes

Code	Calculation
1	$R = X + Y$
2	$R = X - Y$
3	$R = X*Y$
4	$R = X/Y$
5	$R = X^Y$

Problem 1 – Using the ON . . . GOTO statement
Write a program to tabulate the code, the X and Y values, and the results of the calculations shown in Table 5.8.

Use the ON . . . GOTO statement to control which calculation is to be carried out according to its associated code. Draw a flowchart for the program, prepare test data, code and run your BASIC program. Remember the test data must test every branch in your program. You may input the codes and data in any order, that is the first set of data may have a code of, say, 3, the next a code of 1, etc. Compare your program with the one listed in Table A3 (page 149). Suitable test data and calculated values are given in Appendix B (page 159).

5.7 Further use of the TAB function and FOR loops

The TAB function may be used with a variable or expression in the brackets following TAB, for example TAB(I), TAB(P − 1). The program given in Table 5.9 outputs a rectangle of variable dimensions, consisting of L1 dashes for the two lines across and L2 − 2 Is for the two vertical lines.

Table 5.9 Program to output a rectangle

```
5 CLS
10 INPUT "START COLUMN POSITION";P
20 INPUT "LENGTH ACROSS & DOWN";L1,L2
30 PRINT TAB(P-1);
40 REM OUTPUT DASHES ACROSS
50 FOR I=1 TO L1
60    PRINT "-";
70 NEXT I
80 PRINT
90 REM OUTPUT "I"S DOWN
100 FOR I=1 TO L2-2
110    PRINT TAB(P-1);"I";
120    FOR J=1 TO L1-2
130       PRINT " ";
140    NEXT J
150    PRINT "I"
160 NEXT I
170 PRINT TAB(P-1);
180 REM OUTPUT DASHES ACROSS
190 FOR I=1 TO L1
200    PRINT "-";
210 NEXT I
```

Notes on Table 5.9

1 Lines 10 and 20 output a message to the user asking for data to be entered.

2 The PRINT statement in line 30 is terminated by a semi-colon (;); this will cause the *next* PRINT statement that is obeyed to output on to the *same* line.

3 Line 80 is necessary to cause the complete line of L1 dashes to be output.

4 Lines 100 to 160 comprise a FOR loop which has another FOR loop (lines 120–140) wholly within it. The FOR loops are said to be *nested* and this will be discussed further in Chapter 8. For each pass through the outer FOR loop, the inner loop is executed L1–2 times, so that an I is output followed by some spaces and then another I. When line 160 is reached another pass through the outer loop is executed until L2–2 lines, consisting of I spaces I, have been output.

In this case, the use of nested FOR loops could be avoided by replacing lines 110 to 150 by the following statement:

110 PRINT TAB(P − 1); "I"; TAB(L1 − 2 + P); "I"

Figure 5.2 shows a rectangle output by the program when the following data was used:

7
20, 10

```
---------------------
I                   I
I                   I
I                   I
I                   I
I                   I
I                   I
I                   I
I                   I
---------------------
```

Fig. 5.2   Rectangle output from program

that is, twenty dashes were output for the two lines across and eight Is for the two vertical lines.

You should enter the program given in Table 5.9 into your computer and run it with different input data.

Problem 2 – Centring a rectangle
Write another program to output a rectangle of variable width and depth in the centre of the screen. The program is listed in Table A4 (page 149).

6

Functions

6.1 Mathematical functions

Commonly used routines, such as those required for obtaining the
integer part of a number (INT), the logarithm and antilogarithm of
a number (LOG and EXP), and trigonometric functions (e.g. SIN)
are available as library functions in BASIC. Examples of a variety of
these functions will be given in the following sections.

Further background on mathematical functions and problems
involving these are given in *The Pocket Calculator* by L. R. Carter
and E. Huzan (Teach Yourself Books).

6.2 Arguments

Each function name is followed by an expression (the argument) in
brackets. The function operates on the argument, that is, the value
of the expression is used in the standard routine represented by the
function name. For example:

$$100 \ S = SQR(B*B - 4*A*C)$$

will evaluate the square root of the expression in brackets, i.e.
$B^2 - 4AC$, and put the result in cell S.

There may be restrictions regarding the values of the argument
associated with a function. For example, it is not possible to take the
square root of a negative number, therefore the argument used with
SQR must not have a negative value. The TAB function followed by
a semicolon causes characters to be output in the column following
the argument value; therefore, this value must correspond to a

possible column position. A comma in place of the semicolon will have a different effect.

6.3 Using library functions

Library functions are used in LET or PRINT statements on their own or in expressions of any complexity. These expressions may contain further library functions. The evaluation is, as usual, working from the innermost brackets outwards.

6.4 Truncation

The INT function gives the largest integer which is not greater than the argument. Therefore, if the argument is a *positive* number, the decimal places are dropped and the number is said to be truncated after INT has been used. For example:

110 LET B = INT(A)

puts 15 into B if A is 15.36. Remember, A will remain unchanged after the LET statement has been obeyed, so it will still contain 15.36.

However, if A contains −15.36 then the integer placed into B is *not* −15 (since this is larger than −15.36) *but* −16; in this case, B does not contain the truncated value of A.

To obtain the truncated value of a *negative* number, the sign must be removed from the number before the INT function is applied, using the function ABS which takes the absolute value of its argument (i.e. the sign is ignored), and the function SGN used. SGN gives the value of 1 if its argument has a positive value, −1 if its argument has a negative value, and a zero if the value of its argument is zero. For example:

120 LET B = SGN(A)*INT(ABS(A))

multiplies the integer part of the absolute value of A by its sign, so that B will contain the truncated value of A when A is positive or negative. Assuming A contains −15.36, as in the previous example,

then ABS(A) gives 15.36, INT(ABS(A)) gives 15, and
SGN(A)∗INT(ABS(A)) multiplies 15 by −1 giving −15.

6.5   Rounding

Numbers often need to be rounded to a nearest number of decimal
places or to a nearest value in general. Adding 0.5 to a number
before truncating it will cause the number to be rounded to the
nearest integer (whole number). For example:

130 LET B = INT(A + 0.5)

puts 24 in B if A contains, say 24.3, and 25 in B if A contains, say
24.5 or 24.6. The program shown in Table 6.1 illustrates this method
of rounding; angles input in decimals of a degree are output in
degrees and minutes, rounded to the nearest minute.

Table 6.1   Rounding to nearest minute

```
10 INPUT "ANGLE(DEG)";A
20 IF A=0 THEN END
30 D=INT(A)
40 REM ROUND MINS
50 M=INT((A-D)*60+.5)
60 PRINT "ANGLE    DEGS   MINS"
70 PRINT A;TAB(10);D;TAB(17);M
80 GOTO 10
```

To round a number to a certain number of decimal places, you
need to divide the number by a scaling factor before adding 0.5,
truncating, and finally multiplying by the scaling factor. For
example, to round to three decimal places the scaling factor is 0.001:

140 LET P2 = INT(P1/0.001 + 0.5)∗0.001

puts 3.142 into P2 when P1 contains 3.14159.

In general, if the scaling factor is contained in F then an expression may be rounded by using:

INT((*expression*)/F + 0.5)∗F

This will work also if, for example, you wish to round a number to
the nearest 10; in this case, F = 10.

6.6 Square roots

Table 6.2 Use of SGN and SQR

```
5 CLS
10 INPUT "NO OF SETS OF VALUES";N
20 FOR I=1 TO N
30    INPUT "A,B,C";A,B,C
40    R=B*B-4*A*C
50    IF SGN(R)=-1 THEN 90
60    R=SQR(R)
70    PRINT "SQUARE ROOT OF R =";R
80    GOTO 100
90    PRINT "RESULT IS NEGATIVE ";
100   PRINT "FOR    ";A;B;C
110 NEXT I
```

The library function for obtaining a square root is SQR. Remember the argument must not have a negative value. You can use SGN to test the sign, as shown in Table 6.2.

Table 6.3 Calculation of diameters of cylindrical tanks

```
5 INPUT "VOLUME";V
10 PRINT "     VOLUME    HEIGHT    DIAMETER"
20 PRINT "     LTRS.     M.        M."
30 PRINT "     ------    ------    --------"
40 DATA 1,1.25,1.75
60 IF V=0 THEN END
70 PRINT
80 FOR I=1 TO 3
90    READ H
100   D=INT(SQR(V/(1000*3.142*H))*200+.5)/100
110   PRINT TAB(4);V;TAB(15);H;TAB(27);D
120 NEXT I
130 RESTORE
140 GOTO 5
```

The program given in Table 6.3 calculates and outputs the diameter in metres (rounded to two decimal places) of cylindrical tanks, given the volume V (in litres of water) and three standard heights in metres. The formula for the volume of a cylinder of height h and radius r is:

$$V = \pi r^2 h$$

Therefore, the diameter *d* is given by:

$$d = 2r = 2 \sqrt{\frac{V}{\pi h}}$$

In the problem, the three standard heights are given in a DATA statement. For each volume *V* the diameter *D* is calculated and output using each of the three standard heights in turn. Every time the READ H statement (line 90) is obeyed, the next value in the DATA statement is taken. That is, the first time through the FOR loop H is taken to be 1, the second time 1.25, and the third time 1.75. The DATA pointer then needs to be reset to the beginning of the DATA values ready for a further three passes through the FOR loop with the next value of *V*. This is achieved by the RESTORE statement in line 130. Use the program to find the diameter of tanks which have volumes of 500 and 1000 litres (1000 litres = 1 m³). The answers are shown in Table 6.4.

Table 6.4   Output from program given in Table 6.3

VOLUME LTRS.	HEIGHT M.	DIAMETER M.
500	1	.8
500	1.25	.71
500	1.75	.6
1000	1	1.13
1000	1.25	1.01
1000	1.75	.85

6.7   Trigonometric functions

The sine, cosine and tangent of angles are obtained by using the function names SIN, COS and TAN respectively, followed by the angle in brackets (expressed in radians). For example:

100 LET X = COS(B)

will put the cosine of B(radians) in cell X.

Only the inverse tangent (arctangent) is available as the function ATN. This has as the argument the tangent of the required angle. The angle obtained will be in radians.

The following BASIC statements may be used to find angle A in radians given that the sine of the angle is S or the cosine of the angle is C:

```
110 LET A = ATN(S/SQR(1 − S*S))
120 LET A = 3.142/2 − ATN(C/SQR(1 − C*C))
```

Note: You must avoid using the above formulae when S = 1 (required angle is $\pi/2$) or C = 1 (required angle is 0).

You may need to use a combination of these functions and you can do this in one statement. For example, you may be given the three sides of a triangle (a,b,c) and need to find the sines of the angles.

You could use the formula

$$\cos B = (a^2 + c^2 - b^2)/2ac$$

to find the cosine of angle B (and similarly for angles A and C).

If you then want to find the sine of the angles, you could use the following formula

$$\sin B = \sin\left(\tan^{-1}\left(\frac{\sqrt{1 - \cos^2 B}}{\cos B}\right)\right)$$

since $\sin^2 B + \cos^2 B = 1$ and $\tan B = \dfrac{\sin B}{\cos B}$.

Therefore, the following BASIC statements will result in sin B being stored in variable S:

```
40 LET X = (A*A + C*C − B*B)/(2*A*C)
50 LET S = SIN(ATN(SQR(1 − X*X)/X))
```

where the *sides* of the triangle (a,b,c) are stored in the variables A, B and C.

6.8   Logarithms and antilogarithms

The logarithms and antilogarithms of expressions are given by the functions LOG and EXP, respectively. For example, the xth root of a number may be found by dividing the log of the number (y) by x and taking the antilog; this may be expressed as shown in the following BASIC statement:

    100 LET R = EXP(LOG(Y)/X)

After this statement has been obeyed, R will contain the required root.

The function LOG gives the logarithm of its argument to base e; these are known as Naperian (or natural) logarithms. Since,

$$\log_{10} y = \frac{\log_e y}{\log_e 10}$$

the following BASIC statement finds the log of a number (Y) to base 10:

    110 LET T = LOG(Y)/LOG(10)

Similarly, the antilog is found by multiplying the log to base 10 by $\log_e 10$ and taking the antilog of the result as follows:

    120 LET A = EXP(T*LOG(10))

e has the value 2.7182818 to 8 significant figures. The function EXP raises e to the Xth power, where X is its argument. That is, $EXP(X) = e^x$; the use of EXP is illustrated further in the next section.

6.9   Hyperbolic functions

Hyperbolic functions may be expressed in terms of e^x. For example:

$$\sinh x = \frac{1}{2}(e^x - e^{-x})$$

$$\cosh h = \frac{1}{2}(e^x + e^{-x})$$

$$\tanh x = \frac{\sinh x}{\cosh x} = \frac{e^x - e^{-x}}{e^x + e^{-x}}$$

The sinh of the number held in cell X will be placed into cell Y by the following LET statement:

110 LET Y = (EXP(X) − EXP(−X))/2

6.10   TAB function

The TAB function has already been used in several examples. The definition of TAB is summarised below. The TAB function may only be used in PRINT and LPRINT statements to give the next output column position.

TAB (I) spaces to position I on the screen or printer so that output will start in the Ith column. TAB (I) will be ignored if the current output position is beyond column I on the screen or printer.

6.11   Random numbers

Pseudo random numbers may be obtained by the use of the function RND(X). This function chooses a number at random between 0 and 1. This facility can be used in programs to form the basis of chance outcome in games, and to simulate randomness in scientific and business applications.

Because a pseudo random number generator is used, the same sequence of random numbers may be generated every time the program is RUN. If $X = 0$ then the last number generated is repeated; if $X < 0$, the pseudo random number generator is re-seeded using the given value of X, but if $X > 0$ is used then the next random number in the sequence is generated.

The random numbers generated will usually need to be manipulated. For example, to represent the throw of a die, integer values between 1 and 6 need to be randomly generated. This may be done with the following instruction:

100 LET T = INT(6∗RND(3) + 1)

The +1 is required as otherwise the truncated integer would lie between 0 and 5.

When it is required to generate numbers to represent a sample from a uniform distribution a single statement similar to the above will be sufficient. In more advanced cases of simulation, it is often required to sample from a given frequency distribution. A sub-routine suitable for these circumstances is described in Chapter 9.

6.12   User-defined functions

You may define your own functions by using a DEF FNx statement, which has the following format:

line number DEF FNx(*variable*) = *expression*

Each user-defined function must have a unique name within the program as given by FNx, where x is a variable name.

Each function has a dummy argument given by the variable in brackets above. The actual argument used when the function is subsequently referenced in the program will be different from the dummy argument in the function definition. For example, the previous expression used to round a number can now be defined as a function as follows:

50 DEF FNR(A) = INT(A/F + 0.5)*F

This can be used subsequently in the same program to round a number to, say, the nearest 100 and to one decimal place as shown in Table 6.5.

Table 6.5   Program to round numbers

```
10 DEF FNR(A)=INT(A/F+.5)*F
20 READ B,C
30 DATA 650,32.55,649,32.54,651,32.56,0,0
40 IF B=0 THEN END
50 REM ROUND B TO NEAREST 100
60 F=100
70 B1=FNR(B)
80 REM ROUND C TO 1 DECIMAL PLACE
90 F=.1
100 C1=FNR(C)
110 PRINT "B =";B;"B1 =";B1;"C =";C;"C1 =";C1
120 PRINT
130 GOTO 20
```

6.13 Problems

Problem 1 – Radius of circumcircle

Write a program to find the radius of a circular track passing through points which form a triangle. The radius (r) of the circumcircle of a triangle is given by:

$$r = \frac{a}{2\sin A} = \frac{b}{2\sin B} = \frac{c}{2\sin C}$$

where a, b, c and A, B, C are the sides and angles of the triangle.

The program is listed in Table A5 (page 150), and the answer for $a = 452$ metres, $b = 386$ metres and $c = 739$ metres is given in Appendix B (page 159). (*Note*: $\cos B = (a^2 + c^2 - b^2)/2ac$.)

Problem 2 – Volumes of solids

The volume of a solid of uniform cross-sectional area (A) and height (H) is given by:

$$V = A \times H$$

The uniform cross-sectional areas of some common solids are given in Table 6.6 together with their codes.

Table 6.6   Some solids with uniform cross-sectional areas

Code	Solid	Cross-sectional area
1	cuboid	$L \times W$
2	cylinder	$\pi \times R^2$
3	hexagonal bar	$\tfrac{1}{2}\sqrt{27} \times D^2$

L = length W = width R = radius D = length of side

Write a program to calculate the volumes of the solids given in Table 6.6. All dimensions are in cm. The name of the solid is to be held in a DATA statement. Output the name of the solid and its volume. Code 0 can be used to terminate execution of the program. Suitable test data is given in Table 6.7, but include some extra data of your own.

The program is listed in Table A6 (page 150), and the answers, are given in Appendix B (page 159). The program presented in Table A6 allows the user to round the answer using a scaling factor

Table 6.7   Data for 'Volumes of solids' problem

Code	1st dimension (L or R or D)	2nd dimension (W or zero)	Height (H)	Required no. of decimal places
2	4.5	0	1.75	2
3	12.6	0	250	0
1	5.3	7.0	4.2	1

(F) to give the required number of decimal places. Note that the scaling factors for 2, 0 and 1 decimal places are .01, 1 and .1, respectively (see section 6.5).

6.14   Character codes

As explained in Chapter 1, characters and numbers are stored in a computer as binary patterns. Standard binary codes have been established by different organisations. The American Standard Code for Information Interchange (ASCII) has been widely adopted and Appendix C (page 161) gives these codes for the basic 64 character set. Characters can be converted into these codes and *vice versa* by the use of ASC and CHR$ string functions. These and further string functions are described below.

6.14.1   CHR$

This function returns to the character corresponding to a specified ASCII code. For example:

    10 LET A$ = CHR$(66)

The ASCII code for the letter B is 66, so the above statement stores B in A$. Words can be built up by concatenation. For example:

    10 LET A$ = CHR$(66) + CHR$(69)

results in A$ = BE, where 69 is the ASCII code for E.

6.14.2 ASC

This function is the opposite of CHR$ in that it returns the ASCII code number for a specified character. For example:

    10 LET X = ASC("E")

results in X = 69.

If the argument is a string variable the ASCII code of the first character is returned. For example:

     5 LET T$ = "MY COMPUTER"
    10 LET X = ASC(T$)

results in X = 77.

6.14.3 LEN

This function returns the length of a string. For example, adding line 20 below:

    20 LET L = LEN(T$)

would set L = 11 (including the space character between Y and C).

6.14.4 LEFT$, RIGHT$

These functions return the leftmost or rightmost specified number of characters from a string. For example:

    30 LET B$ = LEFT$(T$,2)

returns the leftmost three characters from the string T$, i.e. B$ = MY, similarly,

    40 LET E$ = RIGHT$(T$,8)

leaves E$ = COMPUTER

6.14.5 MID$

This function returns a substring of *n* characters starting with the *i*th character. For example:

    50 LET C$ = MID$(T$,7,3)

results in C$ = PUT where $n = 3$ and $i = 7$

If n is not specified, then the whole of the string from the ith position to the end is returned; for example, if ",3" were omitted in the brackets in line 10 above, then C$ would equal PUTER.

6.14.6   STR$

This function converts a numeric argument to the string equivalent of its PRINTed form. For example:

```
10 LET N = 30
20 LET X$ = STR$(N)
```

results in X$ containing "30" as a string, thus

```
30 LET Y$ = "JAN" + X$
40 PRINT Y$
```

results in,

JAN 30

being printed. Note that the string version of the numeric contains a leading blank (the suppressed + sign).

6.14.7   VAL

This function is the opposite of STR$. The string is examined, left to right, and the *first* recognisable number format is returned unless the first character in the string is non-numeric. For example:

$$X = VAL("30\ JAN") \text{ results in } X = 30$$
but $\quad X = VAL("JAN\ 30") \text{ results in } X = 0$
and $\quad X = VAL("-78.97.65") \text{ results in } X = -78.97$

6.15   The TIME variable

Table 6.8   Clock for two players program

```
10 CLS:P$(0)="0":P$(1)="0"
20 INPUT "TIME LIMIT IN MINS";TL:PRINT
30 INPUT "STARTING COLOUR(W/B)";C$
40 N=INT(ASC(C$)/87):CLS
50 LOCATE 3,7:PRINT "WHITE"
```

```
55 LOCATE 3,21:PRINT "BLACK"
60 TIME$=P$(N)
70 T$=TIME$
80 LOCATE 5,(21-N*14):PRINT T$
90 H=VAL(LEFT$(T$,2))
100 M=VAL(MID$(T$,4,2))
110 S=VAL(RIGHT$(T$,2))
120 IF (H*3600)+(M*60)+S =>TL*60 THEN 170
130 IF INKEY$="" THEN 70
140 P$(N)=T$
150 N=1-N
160 GOTO 60
170 IF N=1 THEN 190
180 LOCATE 7,7:PRINT "WHITE WINS!":END
190 LOCATE 7,7:PRINT "BLACK WINS!":END
```

Table 6.8 shows a program that can be used to time two players' moves for chess. You enter the time-limit in minutes for the players in response to the INPUT statement at line 20; the time-limit is then stored in the variable TL. Then enter W or B to say whether white or black is to start (line 30).

Line 40 is used to calculate N, which will be either 1, if W (character code 87) has been entered, or 0 if B (character code 66) has been entered. The values of N are used later in the program for storing the elapsed time in the appropriate memory cells P$(0) or P$(1) for black or white, respectively. P$(0) and P$(1) are string variables which are set to "0" in line 10. The LOCATE statements (lines 50 and 55) position the cursor at the appropriate row and column locations (the x and y coordinates respectively).

The current time, held in a special variable TIME$ in the form hh:mm:ss (that is, two digits for the hours, minutes and seconds separated by colons), is set to P$(N) in line 60; this means that TIME$ is set to "0" first time through. TIME$ is updated automatically by the computer so that it holds the elapsed time since it was last set. The contents of TIME$ are stored in the variable T$ in line 70.

Lines 70 to 130 form a continuous loop which is left either when a player presses any key on the keyboard (line 130) or when the time-limit is exceeded (line 120). (Note that the function INKEY$ returns a null string if no key is pressed or a one-character string containing a character read from the keyboard, therefore the loop is not left until INKEY$ is not equal to a null string.)

The looping (lines 70–130) causes the 'clock' for the current player to be updated and displayed until this player presses a key. Control then passes to line 140 where the elapsed time for the current player is stored in P$(N) and N takes the alternate value for the other player at line 150 (that is, if N was 1, N becomes 0, and if N was 0, it becomes 1).

The program returns from line 160 to line 60 where TIME$ is set to the *current* player's elapsed time (held in P$(N)). The LOCATE statement (line 80) positions the cursor so that the current player's time (held in T$) is displayed in the appropriate position on the screen.

When either player exceeds the time-limit (as tested in line 120), a branch is made to line 170 to determine the winner. If N is currently 1, this indicates that the time ran out for the white player and black wins (line 190). Similarly, if N is 0, white wins (line 180).

An example of the display, for a time-limit of 5 minutes, is shown in Figure 6.1.

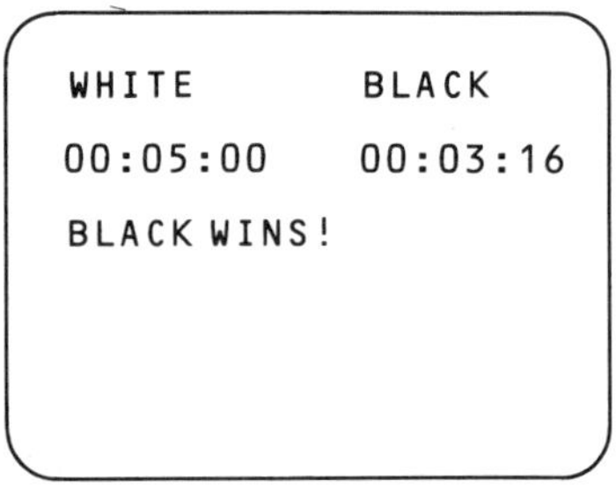

```
WHITE        BLACK

00:05:00     00:03:16

BLACK WINS!
```

Fig. 6.1 Output from clock program

7

Colour and Graphics

7.1 Introduction

This chapter discusses and illustrates the types of colour and graphics features likely to be found on your computer. Each program is designed to demonstrate just one or two features at a time so that the programming logic is clear. The commands and their effects can vary from system to system depending upon the version of BASIC, the microcomputer and the monitor being used. For this reason the programs are also designed for easy experimentation.

The programs demonstrate the range of colours available, the use of text, the graphics mode and graphics commands. A simple use of a macro drawing language incorporated into most BASICs is also presented.

7.2 The range of colours and system

Text characters are displayed in a foreground colour against a coloured background. Monochrome monitors usually show text in green against a black background; colour monitors allow the colour combination to be chosen by the user. In addition there is a colour border around the screen area but as this is often set to the same colour as the screen it is not evident.

The BASIC command for setting the colour combination to be used is:

$$COLOR f,s,b$$

where

f = a numeric value for the foreground (e.g. text)
s = a numeric value for the screen
b = a numeric value for the border

Note the American spelling for COLOR.

Typically there are sixteen possible colours available. Depending upon the quality of the colour monitor being used some colour combinations might be difficult to view or read. The program in Table 7.1 is designed to allow you to experiment with different colour combination for the text, screen and border.

Table 7.1 Demonstration of foreground, screen and border colours

```
10  SCREEN  0,1:F=15:S=4:B=7
20  CLS
30  COLOR F,S,B
40  PRINT
50  PRINT"        COLOR";F;",";S;",";B
60  PRINT"  0 BLACK"
70  PRINT"  1 BLUE"
80  PRINT"  2 GREEN"
90  PRINT"  3 CYAN"
100 PRINT"  4 RED"
110 PRINT"  5 MAGENTA"
120 PRINT"  6 BROWN"
130 PRINT"  7 WHITE"
140 PRINT"  8 GREY"
150 PRINT"  9 LIGHT BLUE"
160 PRINT"10 LIGHT GREEN"
170 PRINT"11 LIGHT CYAN"
180 PRINT"12 LIGHT RED"
190 PRINT"13 LIGHT MAGENTA"
200 PRINT"14 YELLOW"
210 PRINT"15 HIGH INTENSITY WHITE"
220 PRINT
230 PRINT "Foreg'd, Screen, or Border "
240 INPUT "    enter F, S or B ";A$
250 PRINT
260 INPUT "COLOUR NUMBER ";N
270 PRINT
280 IF A$="F" THEN INPUT"BLINK Y/N ";B$
290 IF B$="Y" AND A$="F" THEN N=N+16
300 IF A$="F" THEN F=N
310 IF A$="S" THEN S=N
320 IF A$="B" THEN B=N
330 GOTO 20
```

When the program is run, the sixteen available colours are listed on the screen and you are requested to input a F, S or B to change the colour of the foreground, background (screen) or border respectively.

Line 10 of the program assigns the default values to the variables to be used for the foreground, screen and border colours (F, S and B). This is a precautionary measure as running the program may leave the screen with an unreadable colour combination. Rerunning the program restores the situation. Line 20 clears the screen before each display. Line 30 sets the current colour combination and line 50 displays the values being used. A list of the choices is printed over lines 60 to 210. The change to be made is input at line 240 and the chosen colour at line 260. Lines 270 to 320 ensure that the appropriate variable is changed. The final line, 330, causes the program to loop and redisplay the options in the chosen colours.

There are a number of points to note when running this program. The range of colours and their numeric values may be different for your system. You might therefore need to amend lines 60 to 210 to suit. The ability to 'blink' the text display may not be implemented. If this is so, lines 280, 290 could cause errors and should be omitted. Another variation to note is the action of changing the screen colour. On some systems changing the screen colour causes the complete existing screen to change, on others only the background to subsequent displays are changed. In the latter case changing the border colour often has the effect of causing the complete screen to change.

It could be useful to run the program through all the possible combinations and note down those that seem best for use with your monitor. After leaving this program, to restore the screen to normal, type COLOR 15,0,0:CLS.

7.3 A mosaic pattern

Table 7.2   Coloured mosaic patterns

```
10 DIM C(12),D(12),O(24,24)
20 COLOR 15,0,0:SCREEN 0,1
30 KEY OFF:CLS
40 LOCATE 1,1
50 FOR I=1 TO 12
```

```
60      N=INT(RND(1)*15+1)
70      C(I)=N
80      D(I)=N
90 NEXT I
100 FOR L=1 TO 12
110    D(1)=C(L)
120    FOR P=12 TO 1 STEP -1
130       O(P,L)=D(P)
140       O(25-P,L)=D(P)
150       O(P,25-L)=D(P)
160       O(25-P,25-L)=D(P)
170       D(P)=D(P-1)
180    NEXT P
190 NEXT L
200 PRINT
210 FOR L=2 TO 23
220    PRINT "                    ";
230    FOR P=1 TO 24
240       COLOR O(P,L)
250       PRINT "##";
260    NEXT P
270    PRINT " "
280 NEXT L
290 GOTO 40
```

The program in Table 7.2 demonstrates how the colour for particular printing positions can be held in memory and manipulated to produce, in this case, a symmetrical mosaic pattern on the screen.

This program makes use of *array variables*. Array variables will be more fully described in the next chapter, but a brief explanation will be given here. The number in brackets after a variable, i.e. C(3), can be regarded as a suffix and is called a subscript. C(1), C(2), C(3), C(4), etc., can be used as variable names instead of C1, C2, C3, C4. The advantage is that the number in brackets can be treated as a variable – e.g. C(N) – and the value of N controlled by the program logic. An array with two values within the brackets – e.g. O(3,5) – is known as a two-dimensional array and can be regarded as a table of values where O(3,5) could represent the entry in column 3, row 5. In this program (Table 7.2) the array O(24,24) contains the individual colour values for a mosaic of 24 × 24 tiles. Each array variable represents many values and its size needs to be specified to the computer in a DIM statement (see Chapter 8).

Line 10 of the program specifies the size of the arrays to be used. The colour combination of the screen is set in line 20 and ensures the screen is in text mode for colour. The coloured mosaic tile to be printed to the screen is a keyboard character. Line 40 positions the cursor in the top left-hand corner.

Lines 50 to 90 form a loop that generates a random sequence of twelve colours. The number of the colour, from 1 to 15, is generated in line 60 and it is assigned to the Ith position in the C and D arrays. During the program run the sequence of twelve random colour numbers remains unchanged in C, while the contents of array D are manipulated as required for each successive line.

The loop over lines 100 to 190 manipulates the colour values for the top left-hand quadrant and also places the same value in mirror image positions in the other three quadrants. As L, the line number, is increased by 1, so the first colour to be displayed D(1) is set to

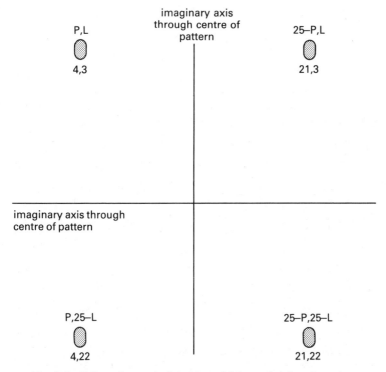

Fig. 7.1 'Mirror images' of positions 4,3 in top left-hand quadrant

C(L). The loop, lines 120 to 180, then allocates the colour values in D to specific positions. Four assignment statements are used to place the contents of D into four mirror image positions in the array O. These positions are illustrated in Figure 7.1. The value 25 occurs in the expression to allow the positions of columns 13–24 to be set up as P varies from 12 to 1. The mirror values will be $25 - 12 = 13$ to $25 - 1 = 24$.

Line 170 advances the colour values along one position, leaving D(1) to contain zero, the value in D(0). On looping back to 110, this first position has a colour value assigned to it, according to the line number, from C(L).

The final part of the program from lines 210 to 280 prints out twenty-two lines, commencing each line with the leading spaces contained in line 220. The loop, lines 230 to 260, then prints out the graphics character twenty-four times, but changing its colour according to the colour value in the array O, position P, line L, i.e. O(P,L). The final line, 290, causes the program to start again. This has the effect of overlaying the existing pattern on the screen with a new, randomly generated pattern.

7.4   Screen modes

On power up the computer would usually be set in text mode. Text mode allows up to 80 characters to be displayed per line although this number might be smaller on home computers. It is also possible to reduce the width of the screen further, i.e. display large characters by use of the WIDTH command. For example list a program on the screen and type:

WIDTH 40

and note the effect. Your computer may use a combination other than 80/40. After noting the effect remember to restore the screen to the full width again by typing WIDTH and the default value.

There are three display modes: text, medium and high-resolution. They are selected by using the statement,

SCREEN *mode*

where mode will be as follows:

0,0   text mode, colour disabled
0,1   text mode, colour enabled
1,0   medium resolution, colour enabled
1,1   medium resolution, colour disabled
2,0   high resolution, no colour available
2,1   ditto

When changing modes by the use of SCREEN either value can be omitted, in which case the most recent value is assumed. However, it is safer to always specify both values when changing modes to avoid confusion.

A screen consists of *pixels*, that is, individual dots or picture elements. The screen resolution is 200 rows of 320 pixels or 200 rows of 640 pixels according to the mode in operation. Medium resolution mode consists of 200 rows of 320 pixels while high resolution uses 200 rows of 640 pixels. In text mode a character consists of 8 by 8 pixels, the screen therefore consists of 200 rows of either 640 or 320 pixels according to the WIDTH command.

The available range of colours can vary according to the screen mode. The full range of colours is usually available in text mode, as demonstrated by the program in Table 7.1 but changing to the other modes to produce graphics often restricts the use of colour. In many systems only two colours are available in high resolution mode. Because of this restriction high resolution mode will not be used in this chapter's programs. However, the effect of using high resolution mode can be seen by changing any program line in this chapter that state SCREEN 1,0 to SCREEN 2.

7.5   Screen 1,0 mode and palette colours

The use of colour in SCREEN 1,0 mode is different from that in text mode. Any background (i.e. screen) colour can be used but the choice of foreground colours is limited to three further colours provided as a group, known as a palette. There are two palettes available, typical colours being:

	PALETTE 0		PALETTE 1
1	Green	1	Cyan

2	Red	2	Magenta
3	Brown	3	White

The colours to be made available are set with the following command:

COLOR *b,p*

where

b = number of the background colour
p = number of the palette, 0 or 1

Note that in graphics mode the background colour is given first whereas in text mode it is given second. Having chosen the palette by using the COLOR command, text will always be displayed in the palette's third colour, i.e. Brown or White.

Graphic commands can use the three colours by reference to their number, 1, 2 or 3 or use the background colour, identified by 0.

The program in Table 7.3 illustrates the use of the COLOR command in SCREEN 1,0 mode. You are asked to choose to work with palette 0 or 1. The program then displays in turn text and three circles filled with the available colours against the sixteen possible coloured backgrounds.

Table 7.3 Palette colours

```
10 CLS:SCREEN 1,0: KEY OFF
20 DIM T$(2,3),B$(16)
30 GOSUB 500
40 GOSUB 600
50 INPUT "PALETTE 0 or 1";P
60 IF P>1 THEN 50
70 FOR B=0 TO 15
80    COLOR B,P
90    CLS
100    PRINT "USING PALETTE ";P
110    PRINT
120    PRINT "TEXT IS ";T$(P,3)
130    PRINT:PRINT
140    FOR C=1 TO 3
150       PRINT "GRAPHICS CAN BE ";T$(P,C);
160       PRINT TAB(30);"=";C
170       PRINT:PRINT
180       CIRCLE (200,20+(24*C)),10,C
190       PAINT (200,20+(24*C)),C,C
```

```
200     NEXT C
210     PRINT
220     PRINT "BACKGROUND IS ";B$(B);" =";B
230     PRINT
240     PRINT
250     PRINT "PRESS SPACE KEY FOR NEXT BACKGROUND ";
260     Z$=INPUT$(1)
270 NEXT B
280 KEY ON:SCREEN 0,1:WIDTH 80
290 END
500 REM SET UP T$
510 DATA "GREEN","RED","BROWN"
520 DATA "CYAN","MAGENTA","WHITE"
530 FOR P=0 TO 1
540     FOR C=1 TO 3
550         READ T$(P,C)
560     NEXT C
570 NEXT P
580 RETURN
600 REM SET UP B$
610 DATA "BLACK","BLUE","GREEN","CYAN","RED"
620 DATA "MAGENTA","BROWN","WHITE","GREY"
630 DATA "LIGHT BLUE","LIGHT GREEN"
640 DATA "LIGHT CYAN","LIGHT RED"
650 DATA "LIGHT MAGENTA","YELLOW"
660 DATA "HIGH INTENSITY WHITE"
670 FOR B=0 TO 15
680     READ B$(B)
690 NEXT B
700 RETURN
```

Line 10 clears the screen, sets the screen mode and turns the prompts for the BASIC function keys off. The text to be displayed is held in two arrays T$ and B$. Line 20 dimensions these arrays and line 30 diverts to the subroutine in line 500 where the T$ array is set up, and then line 40 similarly allows the B$ array to be set up from the subroutine starting in line 600. The required palette to be demonstrated is chosen in line 50.

The loop over lines 70 to 270 displays the screen against the sixteen possible background colours. Line 80 sets up the appropriate background colour and chosen palette and line 90 clears the screen. Text messages are displayed over lines 100 to 130 citing the palette number and text colour. The nested loop 140 to 200 is used to display examples of the three palette colours. Lines 150, 160 print details of the colour number used in drawing and filling the circles produced by lines 180, 190. The CIRCLE and PAINT commands are described later in this chapter. Line 220 displays the current background number. The program pauses at line 260 until a key is pressed. INPUT$(1) causes one keyboard character (the first pressed) to be assigned to Z$.

When all the background colours have been displayed line 280 returns the computer to the default setting. This has the BASIC function key display on, and a text mode screen of 80 characters.

7.6 Graphics on the medium resolution screen

BASIC contains a number of line drawing commands that allow you to produce lines, rectangles and circles on the screen and to fill in bounded areas with colour.

Graphics commands involve specifying pixel positions on the screen. The pixel position is referenced by a pair of *x,y* coordinate values where 0,0 is the top left-hand position on the screen and, for example, 0,199 is the bottom left hand position. In medium resolution mode the bottom right of the screen would be 199,319 and in high resolution mode 199,639.

LINE

The general format of the LINE instruction is:

LINE (X1,Y1) − (X2,Y2),C

where X1,Y1 and X2,Y2 are the coordinates of the beginning and the end of the line respectively. C is the colour number required for the line.

The use of LINE is straightforward, and the programming task really centres around properly controlling the coordinates as variables. Table 7.4 gives a program that draws five overlapping triangles using the line function and illustrates the manipulation of the coordinate variables.

Table 7.4 Program to draw five overlapping triangles

```
10 CLS
20 SCREEN 1,0:COLOR 0,0
30 Y1=50:Y2=80:Y3=120
40 FOR I=1 TO 5
50    LINE (46,Y1)-(150,Y2),I
60    LINE (150,Y2)-(90,Y3),I
70    LINE (90,Y3)-(46,Y1),I
80 Y1=Y1+16:Y2=Y2+16:Y3=Y3+16
90 NEXT I
100 END
```

Line 10 clears the screen and line 20 sets the screen mode. The y coordinate values of the three corners of the triangle are set in line 30 as Y1, Y2, and Y3. Lines 40 to 90 form a loop to produce five triangles. The colour will therefore range from numbers 1 to 5 inclusive. Line 50 plots the top side of the triangle from an x coordinate of 46 to 150. Line 60 plots the right side of the triangle from the last position ($x = 150$) to $x = 90$. Line 70 completes the triangle by going from $x = 90$ back to the original value, $x = 46$. A similar 'rotation' of the y coordinates takes place over lines 50 to 70.

Prior to drawing the next triangle all the y coordinates are increased by sixteen, in line 80. The x coordinates are left the same so the effect is to overlay the triangles vertically down the screen.

Note the effect of drawing five triangles, with the colour number ranging from 1 to 5, when only three colours are available.

PAINT
The function PAINT fills in a bounded area with a specified colour and is used as:

PAINT (X,Y),C

where X,Y are the starting coordinates (and must be within the bounded area), and C is the colour to be used (and should correspond to the existing boundary colour).

The program in Table 7.4 can be modified to cause the triangles to be filled in with their colours. To achieve this, another coordinate position needs to be created as a variable that is inside the bounded area. Three new lines need to be added, i.e.

```
35 Z = 115
75 PAINT (90,Z),C
85 Z = Z + 16
```

By setting Z to 115 in line 35, the PAINT coordinate 90,115 will be within the first triangle drawn. Line 85 moves the point in step with the new position of each triangle. This movement is shown in Figure 7.2.

It is important that the starting position for the PAINT command is correct. For some applications the starting position is not a preset coordinate and needs to be calculated by the program to ensure it is

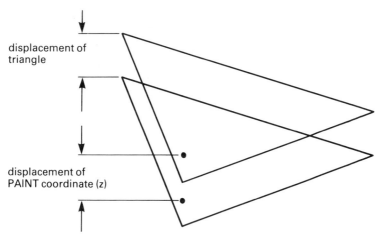

Fig. 7.2　Displacement of PAINT coordinate in step with triangle

within the correct bounded area. This may require a good knowledge of geometry as demonstrated in a later program, Table 7.7 (page 66).

Rectangles

The line function can be used to create rectangles by terminating it with a B, for example:

LINE (X1,Y1) – (X2,Y2),C,B

In this case, the coordinates are interpreted as diagonally opposite corners of a rectangle.

If BF is used instead of B, the rectangle is filled using the specified colour, C. The program in Table 7.5 illustrates the use of LINE to produce overlapping coloured rectangles.

Table 7.5　Program to draw overlapping coloured rectangles

```
10 CLS
20 SCREEN 1,0:COLOR 0,0
30 X=10:Y=0
40 FOR I=1 TO 5
50     X=X+30:Y=Y+15
60     LINE(X,Y)-(X+80,Y+100),I,BF
70 NEXT I
80 END
```

The first three lines initialise the colours, the screen mode and the *x,y* coordinates. Lines 40 to 70 set up a loop to draw five rectangles. On each successive pass through the loop the top left-hand corner coordinates are increased by thirty on the *x* axis and fifteen on the *y* axis. The rectangle is drawn and filled in in line 60. The diagonally opposite corner is across 80 on the *x* axis and down 100 on the *y* axis. Once again, notice the effect of going beyond palette colour number 3 within the loop.

CIRCLE

The circle function allows arcs, circles and ellipses to be drawn on the screen. The general form for CIRCLE is:

CIRCLE (X,Y),R,C,S,F,A

where

X,Y are the coordinates of the centre
R is the radius
C is the colour
S is the start angle (in radians)
F is the finish angle (in radians)
A is the aspect ratio of an ellipse

The aspect ratio is the ratio of the vertical axis to the horizontal axis. For the case of an ellipse the radius relates to the *x* axis. You should omit A (and the preceding comma) to obtain a circle.

As the start and finish angles are specified in radians, it is necessary to ensure that any values calculated within a program do not exceed 6.28 (i.e. 2π). Angles in degrees can be converted to radians for practical purposes by multiplying by the factor 6.28/360, for example:

90 degrees = 90*6.28/360 radians

A program that draws and paints a collection of ellipses is given in Table 7.6. Line 10 clears the screen, and line 20 sets the screen mode. The centre of the ellipses is set at X = 150, Y = 100 in line 30 and the radius initialised to 100. The loop over lines 40 to 70 produces three ellipses. Each time round the loop the radius is reduced by ten (line 50) and the ellipse drawn by line 60. A complete

Table 7.6   Program to draw and paint ellipses

```
10 CLS
20 SCREEN 1,0:COLOR 0,0
30 X=150:Y=100:R=100
40 FOR I=1 TO 3
50    R=R-10
60    CIRCLE(X,Y),R,I,0,6.28,.5
65    PAINT(X,Y),I
70 NEXT I
80 END
```

ellipse is drawn because the starting and finishing angles are between 0 and 2π radians. Ellipses are drawn because an aspect ratio has been set, in this case 0.5. The ellipses are filled in by the PAINT function in line 65, using their centres as the starting point.

If the start or finish angle is specified as negative, a line is also drawn from the centre to the end of the arc. The following would therefore produce a quadrant (i.e. 90 degree segment of a circle):

CIRCLE (100,100),80,8 − 0, − 90*6.28/360

An example of using the CIRCLE function to draw quadrants is given in the next section which describes a program to produce a pie chart.

7.7   A pie chart example

This example combines the use of graphic functions with text to produce a 3-segment coloured pie chart representing percentages entered by the user. The program is given in Table 7.7.

Table 7.7   Coloured pie chart example

```
10 CLS:KEY OFF
20 SCREEN 1,0: COLOR 0,1
30 REM KEYBOARD ENTRY STAGE
40 PRINT "ENTER 3 PERCENTAGE SEGMENTS"
50 PRINT
60 INPUT "% 1ST SEGMENT ";S1
70 INPUT "% 2ND SEGMENT ";S2
80 INPUT "% 3RD SEGMENT ";S3
90 P1=S1:P2=S2:P3=S3
100 IF S1+S2+S3=100 THEN 150
110 PRINT
120 PRINT "% DO NOT TOTAL 100, TRY AGAIN"
130 PRINT:PRINT:GOTO 40
140 REM RADIAN CALCULATIONS
```

```
150 CLS
160 S1=S1*6.28/100:S2=S2*6.28/100:S3=S3*6.28/100
170 S1=S1
180 IF S1>6.28 THEN S1=S1-6.28
190 S2=S1+S2
200 IF S2>6.28 THEN S2=S2-6.28
210 S3=S2+S3
220 IF S3>6.28 THEN S3=S3-6.28
230 REM PLOT SEGMENTS
240 CIRCLE (160,100),90,1,-6.28,-S1
250 CIRCLE (160,100),90,1,-S1,-S2
260 CIRCLE (160,100),90,1,-S2,-6.28
270 REM FILL SEGMENTS
280 CX=160+(COS((0+S1)/2))*45
290 CY=100-(SIN((0+S1)/2))*45
300 PAINT (CX,CY),1,1
310 TX1=CX/8:TY1=CY/8
320 CX=160+(COS((S1+S2)/2))*45
330 CY=100-(SIN((S1+S2)/2))*45
340 PAINT (CX,CY),2,1
350 TX2=CX/8:TY2=CY/8
360 CX=160+(COS((S2+6.28)/2))*45
370 CY=100-(SIN((S2+6.28)/2))*45
380 PAINT (CX,CY),3,1
390 TX3=CX/8:TY3=CY/8
400 REM ADD TEXT
410 LOCATE TY1,TX1
420 PRINT P1;"%"
430 LOCATE TY2,TX2
440 PRINT P2;"%"
450 LOCATE TY3,TX3
460 PRINT P3;"%"
470 END
```

Line 10 clears the screen and turns the BASIC function key prompts off. The screen mode and palette is set in line 20. Lines 40 to 130 is the keyboard entry routine. Three percentage segments, S1, S2 and S3, are input over lines 60 to 80. Their values are transferred into P1, P2 and P3 respectively in line 90 to be retained for subsequent text output. If the three percentages add up to 100% then line 100 bypasses the error message in line 120 and continues the program execution at line 150.

Line 150 clears the screen ready to display the chart. The percentages are converted into radian measure in line 160 and S1, S2 and S3 are then further converted into the cumulative radians over lines 170 to 220. Lines 180, 200 and 220 are a precaution to ensure that the radian values do not exceed a complete circle (i.e. $2*\pi$, which equals 6.28).

The three segments are plotted over lines 240 to 260 with a radius of 90. At this stage the screen consists of a circle divided in proportion to the original percentages input. The next stage is to calculate a suitable position from which to invoke the PAINT function and to locate the text for each segment. Line 280 calculates the position of a horizontal coordinate. This is done by calculating the cosine of the mid-point between the two radians and multiplying by half the radius. The result is the horizontal component of the vector that bisects the segment at half the radius from a theoretical circle centred on 0,0. The final step in line 280 is to add this component to the horizontal coordinate of the plotted circle, i.e. 160. Line 290 similarly calculates the vertical component and adds it to the centre position. The PAINT function is then invoked from this position at line 300 to fill the first segment with colour 1 of the palette. Line 310 converts the horizontal pixel position, CX into a text location position, TX1, as each text position uses 8 pixels. The same line also calculates TY1, the vertical text location position.

The other two segments are filled and their text positions calculated in a similar manner over lines 320 to 390. Finally the percentages are printed in text form over each segment in lines 410 to 460.

7.8   Macro drawing language

BASICs often have a macro drawing language that allows a sequence of drawing commands to be contained in a string variable. A string variable can therefore define an object or shape which is drawn when the DRAW statement is executed.

The following movement commands can be built into a string variable, *n* is the distance moved:

U *n*   move up
D *n*   move down
L *n*   move left
R *n*   move right
E *n*   move diagonally up and right
F *n*   move diagonally down and right
G *n*   move diagonally down and left
H *n*   move diagonally up and left

M*x,y*   move to coordinates *x,y*

M + *x,y* or M − *x,y*   move relative to current position

B   move, but don't plot

N   move, but return to original position

A *n*   rotates direction of movement

    0 degrees where *n* = 0

   90 degrees where *n* = 1

 180 degrees where *n* = 2

 270 degrees where *n* = 3

C *n*   sets the colour

S *n*   sets scale factor, where factor = *n*/4 and *n* can be from 0 to 255. For example, if *n* = 1 then the scale factor is 1/4. Note that 'no-scaling' occurs when *n* = 4 and also for the default value of *n* = 0.

The above commands can be assigned to a string variable, for example:

    F$ = "R100D80L100U80"

Thus F$ contains 'instructions' to draw a rectangle 100 by 80 pixels. If the scale factor were set to 1/2 then the rectangle would be 50 by 40 pixels. A DRAW command is used to have F$ executed, for example:

    DRAW "XF$;"

In this format the X within the string (i.e. quotes) indicates that a substring, F$, should be executed. Note that a ; terminates the string.

A program to demonstrate some of the DRAW commands is given in Table 7.8. This program draws a simple house with a roof, four windows and a door.

Table 7.8   Program to draw a house

```
10 CLS
20 SCREEN 1,0:COLOR 0,7
30 F$="R100D80L100U80"
40 W$="R20D15L20U15"
50 D$="R10D30L10U30"
60 R$="E15R70F15"
70 T$="BM+10,10"+W$
80 T$=T$+"BM+60,0"+W$
```

```
 90 L$="BM-60,40"+W$
100 L$=L$+"BM+60,0"+W$
110 DRAW "BM50,50"
120 DRAW "XF$;"
130 DRAW "XT$;"
140 DRAW "XL$;"
150 DRAW "BM-25,0"
160 DRAW "XD$;"
170 DRAW "BM50,50"
180 DRAW "XR$;"
190 END
```

Line 20 sets up the colour and the medium resolution screen. Line 30 defines a large rectangle for the frame of the house in F$. A window is defined in line 40 as W$, a door in line 50 as D$ and the roof in line 60 as R$.

Line 70 defines a string T$, for the first window of the top floor. BM + 10,10 causes the window, W$, to be positioned ten units down and to the right of the top corner of the frame. Line 80 adds onto the existing definition of T$ a horizontal move of 60 and a further window.

A string for the lower floor, L$, is defined in a similar manner. Line 90 positions the cursor by coming back 60 and going down 40 and places a window. Line 100 adds a second window to the definition.

The first DRAW command, line 110, positions the cursor then line 120 draws the frame. Line 130 draws the top windows, line 140 the lower windows. The cursor is then positioned, in line 150, for drawing the door in line 160. Finally the cursor is positioned back to the start by line 170 and the roof drawn in line 180.

To test the working of this program it is suggested that you run it with some DRAW commands omitted. For example, initially omit lines 130 to 180, then progressively add lines 130 to 180 to obtain the complete house.

8

Arrays

8.1 Lists and tables

So far single memory cells have been referenced by single variable names.

Many problems involve processing a number of variables in exactly the same way. In these programs, it is much more convenient to use the same name to reference a number of memory cells whose contents are processed by the same set of instructions in the program; a subscript is used in association with the variable name to identify uniquely each particular memory cell. For example, the program given in Table 8.1 inputs a list of N numbers and outputs a list of numbers that are greater than 10, and a list of numbers that are negative, using two passes through the stored data.

Table 8.1 Program to output numbers > 10 and negative numbers

```
10 INPUT "NO OF NUMBERS";N
20 FOR I=1 TO N
30     INPUT "NUMBER";A(I)
40 NEXT I
50 CLS:PRINT "NUMBERS > 10":PRINT
60 FOR I=1 TO N
70     IF A(I) <= 10 THEN 90
80     PRINT A(I)
90 NEXT I
100 PRINT:PRINT
110 PRINT "NEGATIVE NUMBERS"
120 PRINT
130 FOR I=1 TO N
140     IF A(I) >= 0 THEN 160
150     PRINT A(I)
160 NEXT I
170 PRINT
```

If N is equal to 9, then the list of 9 numbers is input into memory cells A(1), A(2), . . . , A(9), since in the FOR loop (lines 20–40) I takes the values 1–9. I is the subscript and A is the name of an array of nine elements. Each element of the array may be referenced by the array name and the subscript referring to its position in the array. That is, A(4) refers to the fourth number input into the array A, which is the memory cell between those occupied by A(3) and A(5).

Generally, your BASIC system will start numbering the elements of an array at 0, that is, the first element of the array is referenced by A(0). The program given in Table 8.1 may be amended so that it can be used to input and process nine numbers starting at A(0) by changing the initial value of I to 0 in each FOR statement, lines 20, 70 and 140. N would need to be input as 8 instead of 9 in this case.

Try running the program given in Table 8.1 with the following nine numbers:

6, 12, −30, 10, −4, 47, 9, 0, 58

The output for this data is shown in Table 8.2.

Table 8.2   Output from program given in Table 8.1

```
NUMBERS > 10
  12
  47
  58
NEGATIVE NUMBERS
−30
−4
```

Array A, in the previous example, is called a one-dimensional array because it has one subscript. A one-dimensional array is a list, and a two-dimensional array is a table. A three-dimensional array is more difficult to visualise; an example would be to have the page number of a book as the third dimension (subscript), and the lines and columns on a page forming a table referenced by the other two subscripts. The subscripts are separated by commas within the brackets following the name of the array, so that T$(3,2,8) could refer to the third line and second column on the eighth page of a book.

8.2 Naming arrays

Arrays used for holding numbers must be called by a variable name followed by the subscripts in brackets.

Array names which are identical to single variable names may be used in the same program. That is, the BASIC system will distinguish between A used as a single variable and A (subscript(s)) used as an array element for storing numbers, and A$ used as a single string variable and A$ (subscript(s)) used for storing character strings.

8.3 Subscripts

The subscripts that may be used with array names may consist of any expression. However, since the subscripts refer to unique positions in the array which is stored in memory cells in the computer, the individual subscripts must be zero or positive integer values.

The integer values of the subscripts must lie within the bounds of the array. For example, in the program given in Table 8.1 the BASIC system automatically allocates eleven memory cells (subscripts 0–10) in the absence of a DIM statement, which will be explained in the next section. If N were input as, say, 20, then elements referenced in the FOR statement beyond the A(10) element would be outside the defined storage of the array (i.e. outside the bounds of the array); in this case an execution error would occur.

8.4 The DIM statement

The DIM statement is used to define storage for arrays which have subscripts whose values are greater than ten. Although the DIM statements can appear anywhere in the program (before the array is accessed) it is better to place it at the beginning of the program so that it is separate from the main logic.

The format of the DIM statement is:

line number DIM list of array variables separated by commas

The array variables in the list may be ordinary or string variables; each variable name is followed by subscripts, separated by commas, in brackets.

For example, array X is to be used to store a list of up to fifty numbers, and array T$ is to be used to hold a table comprising a maximum of 5 rows and 7 columns.

The DIM statement to define storage for these two arrays is:

    30 DIM X(50), T$(5,7)

X will have fifty-one memory cells of storage reserved, referenced by X(0), X(1), X(2), . . . , X(50). T$ will have a total of forty-eight cells reserved, the first cell being referenced by T$(0,0) and the last cell by T$(5,7).

Notice that storage is reserved for the *maximum* array size in each case. A particular run of your program may require less storage than the maximum and this is acceptable.

More than one DIM statement may be used in a program, but the *same* array name may *not* appear in more than one DIM statement in a program. For example:

    50 DIM B$(30,8),A$(60),A(20,20) ⎫
    60 DIM D(100), C$(5,7,6)   ⎬ correct
                                    ⎭

is correct.

    70 DIM B$(30,8),A$(60),A(20,20)   ⎫
    80 DIM D(100),A(15,15),C$(5,7,6) ⎬ incorrect
                                      ⎭

will produce an error because A(20,20) appears in the DIM statements in line 70 and A(15,15) in the DIM statement in line 80.

However, if line 75 is inserted as follows, then the dimensioning will be correct because array A will have been erased before it is redimensioned.

    75 ERASE A

Note that several arrays may be eliminated from a program by specifying them as a list in the ERASE statement, and the memory space allocated to the arrays can then be reused.

It is important to note that the DIM statement may be used to override the automatic storage allocation for small arrays. For example, if array A is to contain a maximum of six cells and array B a maximum of four cells, then DIM A(5),B(3) will cause the *exact* storage required to be allocated, thus *saving* storage compared with the automatic allocation of eleven cells for each array.

8.5 Nested FOR loops

A FOR loop may lie wholly within another FOR loop, as was shown in Table 5.9 (page 36). This facility is particularly useful for manipulating arrays. For example, the data given in Table 8.3 is to be input into a two-dimensional array called A and output in the form shown in Table 8.4. The program given in Table 8.5 uses nested FOR loops to achieve this; try running this program.

Table 8.3 Input data for 'Nested FOR loops' program

1	2	3	4
5	6	7	8
9	10	11	12

Table 8.4 Table to be output

1	5	9
2	6	10
3	7	11
4	8	12

Table 8.5 Program using nested FOR loops

```
10 DIM A(3,4)
20 DATA 1,2,3,4,5,6,7,8,9,10,11,12
30 FOR I=1 TO 3
40    FOR J=1 TO 4
50       READ A(I,J)
60    NEXT J
70 NEXT I
80 FOR I-1 TO 4
90    FOR J=1 TO 3
100      PRINT A(J,I);
110   NEXT J
120   PRINT
130 NEXT I
```

8.6 Problems

Write programs for the following problems.

Problem 1 – Copying an array

Copy an array A comprising N elements into an array B, of the same size as A, in reverse order. For example, if N is 20, A(20) will go into B(1), A(19) into B(2), etc. Assume N is always a multiple of 5, and output array B in rows of 5 columns.

The program is listed in Table A7 (page 151).

Problem 2 – Sum of elements

Sum the elements on the diagonals of an M × M array. Allow for M to be odd (as well as even) when the central element must be added in only *once*. Test your program with an odd *and* an even value of M. Output the array and the sum of the elements on the diagonals in each case.

The program is listed in Table A8 (page 151).

Problem 3 – Sorting a list of numbers

Sort a list of N numbers, held in array A, into ascending numerical order. Use only *one* array which is *just* large enough to hold the maximum number of numbers that may be input. The logic of the method is shown in Figure 8.1. This involves pushing the highest number to the end of the list by exchanging the higher number of each pair working through the list. That is, if element A(1) is greater than element A(2) then their contents are exchanged so that the higher value is in A(2); then the value in A(2) is compared with that in A(3) and exchanged if necessary. The second pass through the list is shorter since at the end of the first pass A(N) contained the highest value in the list and does not need to be compared again. If no exchanges take place during a pass (i.e. E = 0) then the list is in the required sorted order and no further passes are necessary.

Output the list of numbers in its original order and after each pass of the sort so that you can see how this sorting method works. Use the following data, and create your own data, to provide a variety of different lists to be sorted.

Data:

$$5, 3, 20, 22, 22, 9, 4, 23, 2, 0, -2$$

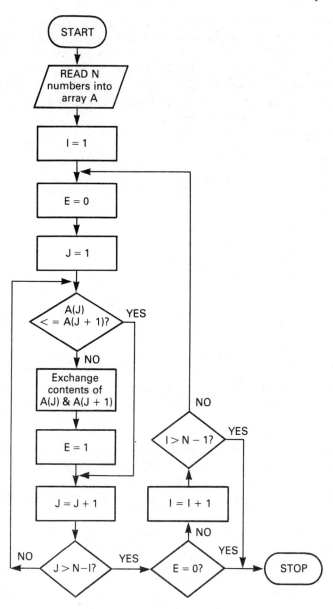

Fig. 8.1 Sorting a list of numbers into ascending order

You can use the SWAP command to exchange the contents of two variables (two array elements, in this case), e.g. SWAP A(J),A(J + 1).

The program is listed in Table A.9 (page 152).

The changes in the order of the numbers in the list after each pass are shown in Table 8.6, starting with the list in its original order and finishing with the numbers sorted in ascending sequence.

Table 8.6 Sorting a list of numbers

5	3	20	22	22	9	4	23	2	0	−2
3	5	20	22	9	4	22	2	0	−2	23
3	5	20	9	4	22	2	0	−2	22	23
3	5	9	4	20	2	0	−2	22	22	23
3	5	4	9	2	0	−2	20	22	22	23
3	4	5	2	0	−2	9	20	22	22	23
3	4	2	0	−2	5	9	20	22	22	23
3	2	0	−2	4	5	9	20	22	22	23
2	0	−2	3	4	5	9	20	22	22	23
0	−2	2	3	4	5	9	20	22	22	23
−2	0	2	3	4	5	9	20	22	22	23

9

Subroutines

9.1   Purpose of subroutines

A subroutine is a sequence of instructions designed to perform one or more specific tasks. The routine may be required more than once in different places in the program. When a routine is written as a subroutine it is incorporated in the main program once. During execution the statement, GOSUB *linenumber*, causes control to pass to the line number specified. Execution continues until a RETURN statement is encountered. Control then passes back to the statement *following* the originating GOSUB statement.

A subroutine can be entered as many times as required and therefore can save the writing of similar instructions in several parts of the program. Apart from the extra program writing, the program usually becomes longer if subroutines are not used. A longer program requires more computer storage, and takes longer to translate into machine code; using subroutines wherever possible generally makes a program more efficient.

Once a subroutine has been developed and tested it may be used in quite different programs, either as it stands or with modifications. If possible, subroutines should be designed to allow them to be used in many different ways without modification. This may be done by building in flexibility.

9.2   Independent development

Another advantage of using subroutines is that they may be developed and tested independently from the program(s) in which they are to be used.

By testing subroutines independently a complex program may be built up more quickly using *proved* subroutines. In addition, if a subroutine has been developed for one program, then it can be tested with suitable test data for use in a different program *before* it is incorporated. However, the final program will need to be tested as a *whole* to ensure that the linkages – i.e. statements between the subroutines (as well as the subroutines) – give correct results for every branch of the program. The test data must be comprehensive enough to test *every* instruction in the program, as discussed in Chapter 4.

9.3   Graphs and histograms

If you use a computer to analyse data it is almost certain that at some time you will want to plot the data, or maybe group it into a frequency table. The following sections describe a series of subroutines that allow you to do this. To allow the subroutines to be compatible we need to standardise some of the variable names. The routines have been written to allow up to 100 data values to be processed. These values will be held in the array V. There is therefore the need for a DIM V(100) in the main program. If the data is to be grouped into a frequency table before, say, printing out a histogram, the variable will be stored in array X and the frequency in array F. A frequency table having a maximum of fifteen class intervals should be adequate for most purposes. Therefore the main program will need a DIM statement containing X(15), F(15).

9.4   Serial plotting routine

A routine to plot a series of values sequentially is useful for time series based data. The examination of the graph might confirm that it is not worthwhile using more elaborate analyses to seek non-existent trends, or seasonal patterns.

A plotting routine is given in Table 9.1. The largest value to be plotted (M) is found (lines 1110–1150) and from this the scaling factor is calculated. Line 1160 has been written to fit the maximum value within thirty print positions. The first ten print positions are taken up by the data point number (N) and the actual value V(I).

Table 9.1 Serial plotting routine

```
1010 PRINT
1020 PRINT "NO OF DATA POINTS =";N
1030 PRINT
1040 INPUT "ENTER NO OF POINTS TO PLOT";Q
1050 IF Q>N THEN 1010
1060 B=1
1070 IF Q=N THEN 1110
1080 PRINT
1090 INPUT "START PLOT AT DATA POINT NO";B
1100 Q=Q+B-1
1110 M=0
1120 FOR I=B TO Q
1130    IF V(I)<M THEN 1150
1140    M=V(I)
1150 NEXT I
1160 S=1+INT(M/30)
1170 PRINT
1180 PRINT "ONE PLOT POSITION =";S;"UNITS"
1190 PRINT
1200 PRINT "N DATA";
1210 PRINT TAB(9);"0";TAB(17);10*S;TAB(27);20*S
1220 PRINT TAB(9);"I....:....I....:....I....:...."
1230 FOR I=B TO Q
1240    K=INT(V(I)/S+.5)
1250    IF K>0 THEN 1290
1260    PRINT MID$(STR$(I),2);TAB(6);MID$(STR$(V(I)),2);
1270    PRINT TAB(9);"*"
1280    GOTO 1310
1290    PRINT MID$(STR$(I),2);TAB(6);MID$(STR$(V(I)),2);
1300    PRINT TAB(9);"I";TAB(K+9);"*"
1310 NEXT I
1320 PRINT TAB(9);"I....:....I....:....I....:...."
1330 PRINT
1340 RETURN
```

Table 9.2 Pastureland in a parish

Year	% Pastureland
1	82
2	72
3	63
4	60
5	57
6	54
7	50
8	45
9	38
10	35

Problem 1 – Plot of percentage pastureland

Write a program using the above routine to plot the reducing percentage pastureland, as given in Table 9.2 (page 81). The program is given in Table A10 (page 152), and the output in Table 9.3.

Table 9.3   Percentage pastureland output

```
ENTER NO OF YEARS? 10

% PASTURELAND, YR  1 ? 82
% PASTURELAND, YR  2 ? 72
% PASTURELAND, YR  3 ? 63
% PASTURELAND, YR  4 ? 60
% PASTURELAND, YR  5 ? 57
% PASTURELAND, YR  6 ? 54
% PASTURELAND, YR  7 ? 50
% PASTURELAND, YR  8 ? 45
% PASTURELAND, YR  9 ? 38
% PASTURELAND, YR 10 ? 35

NO OF DATA POINTS = 10

ENTER NO OF POINTS TO PLOT? 10

NO OF DATA POINTS = 10

ENTER NO OF POINTS TO PLOT? 10

ONE PLOT POSITION = 3 UNITS

N DATA   O          30          60
         I....:....I....:....I....:....
  1   82 I                              *
  2   72 I                         *
  3   63 I                    *
  4   60 I                   *
  5   57 I                  *
  6   54 I                 *
  7   50 I               *
  8   45 I             *
  9   38 I         *
 10   35 I        *
         I....:....I....:....I....:....
```

9.5   Frequency grouping subroutines

Before producing a histogram, or carrying out other forms of analysis, it is often required to group individual data points into class intervals and note the total number of values falling into each interval (i.e. the frequency).

A subroutine to do this is given in Table 9.4. The frequency table so constructed is composed of fifteen class intervals. Any data not included as a result of this constraint is printed out by line 2090. A new run can then be undertaken with the class interval parameters respecified accordingly.

The reason for designing the program in this manner is that a completely automatic parameter setting routine may disguise the presence of a 'rogue' value which, once pointed out, you are happy to ignore.

Table 9.4 Frequency grouping routine

```
2000 INPUT "SIZE OF CLASS INTERVAL";C
2010 PRINT
2020 INPUT "LOWER BOUND OF 1ST. INTERVAL";L
2030 FOR I=1 TO N
2040    FOR J=1 TO 15
2050       IF V(I) >= (L+(C*J)) THEN 2080
2060       F(J)=F(J)+1
2070       GOTO 2100
2080    NEXT J
2090    PRINT V(I);"NOT COUNTED"
2100 NEXT I
2110 FOR J=1 TO 15
2120    X(J)=L+((J-.5)*C)
2130 NEXT J
2140 RETURN
```

Table 9.5 Frequency table routine

```
3000 PRINT
3010 C=X(2)-X(1)
3020 L=X(1)-(.5*C)
3030 PRINT "-------------------"
3040 PRINT TAB(6);"X";TAB(16);"F"
3050 PRINT "-------------------"
3060 FOR I=1 TO 15
3070    B=L+C*(I-1)
3080    PRINT B;TAB(6);"-";TAB(16);F(I)
3090 NEXT I
3100 PRINT "-------------------"
3110 RETURN
```

A subroutine to print out a frequency table is given in Table 9.5. As this subroutine is intended to be independent of the grouping subroutine, the class interval and lower bounds are calculated from the array values of X.

The third subroutine in this set outputs the frequency table in histogram form. The program is given in Table 9.6. As with the plotting routine it has been written to use thirty print positions for the histogram.

Table 9.6   Histogram routine

```
4000 M=F(1)
4010 PRINT
4020 PRINT
4030 FOR I=2 TO N
4040    IF F(I) < M THEN 4060
4050    M=F(I)
4060 NEXT I
4070 IF M > 30 THEN 4120
4080 U=INT(30/M)
4090 S=1/U
4100 PRINT U;" STARS = 1 UNIT"
4110 GOTO 4140
4120 S=INT(M/30)+1
4130 PRINT "ONE STAR = ";S;" UNITS"
4140 PRINT
4150 PRINT "CLASS";
4160 PRINT TAB(5);"I....:....I....:....I....:....I"
4170 FOR I=1 TO 15
4180    K=INT((F(I)/S)+.5)
4190    IF K > 0 THEN 4220
4200    PRINT I;TAB(5);"I"
4210    GOTO 4270
4220    PRINT I;TAB(5);"I";
4230    FOR J=1 TO K
4240       PRINT "*";
4250    NEXT J
4260    PRINT
4270 NEXT I
4280 PRINT TAB(5);"I....:....I....:....I....:....I"
4290 PRINT
4300 RETURN
```

Problem 2 – Pastureland histogram

Write a program incorporating these subroutines to process the data shown in Table 9.7. The output required is a frequency table and histogram of the percentage pastureland.

The program, which gives the output shown in Tables 9.8 (page 85) and 9.9 (page 86), is listed in Table A11 (page 152). Use CONT when running the program to display the two tables.

Table 9.7   Parish data

Parish	% amount of pastureland
1	46
2	47
3	63
4	74
5	76
6	26
7	37
8	39
9	35
10	43
11	52
12	59

Table 9.8   Frequency table for Problem 2

X	F
20 –	1
30 –	3
40 –	3
50 –	2
60 –	1
70 –	2
80 –	0
90 –	0
100 –	0
110 –	0
120 –	0
130 –	0
140 –	0
150 –	0
160 –	0

Table 9.9   Histogram for Problem 2

```
10   STARS = 1 UNIT

CLASS
      I....:....I....:....I....:....I
   1  I**********
   2  I********************************
   3  I*********************************
   4  I********************
   5  I**********
   6  I*******************
   7  I
   8  I
   9  I
  10  I
  11  I
  12  I
  13  I
  14  I
  15  I
      I....:....I....:....I....:....I
```

9.6   Sampling from a frequency distribution

A subroutine is described below that allows a value to be sampled from a frequency distribution. The frequency distribution is contained in the two-dimensional array X. The first dimension contains the variable value, the second dimension contains the cumulative percentage frequency.

To allow the subroutine to be used generally in a variety of programs some standardisation of the array containing the frequency distribution is necessary. The number of class intervals has been set at 10 resulting in the dimensions for the array X being (10,2). Note that, for convenience, the existence of 0 subscripts has been ignored. If a required distribution contains less than ten rows

Table 9.10   Data to be sampled

Variable	Cumulative % frequency
5	10
10	27
15	42
20	65
25	80
30	100

(i.e. class intervals), the final entries in the array will be identical. For example, the data to be sampled, shown in Table 9.10, would be contained in the array X(R,I) as shown in Table 9.11.

Table 9.11 Contents of X(R,I)

		Column subscript, I	
		(,1)	*(,2)*
	(1,)	5	10
	(2,)	10	27
	(3,)	15	42
	(4,)	20	65
	(5,)	25	80
Row subscript, R	(6,)	30	100
	(7,)	30	100
	(8,)	30	100
	(9,)	30	100
	(10,)	30	100

Any distributions to be used from a main program are established in a similar (10,2) format and array X can be equated to them before entering the subroutine.

9.7 Description of subroutine

A flowchart for the subroutine is shown in Figure 9.1 (page 88) and the listing is given in Table 9.12.

Table 9.12 Sampling routine

```
900 REM SAMPLING SUB
910 Z=100*RND(3)
920 FOR R=1 TO 10
930    V=X(R,1)
940    IF Z <+ X(R,2) THEN 980
950 NEXT R
960 PRINT "ERROR:RN NOT PROPERLY ALLOCATED"
970 END
980 RETURN
```

The random number generated is scaled to lie between 0 and 100 (line 910). Within the FOR loop the array X is inspected row by row. The value of the current row variable is assigned to V (line 930)

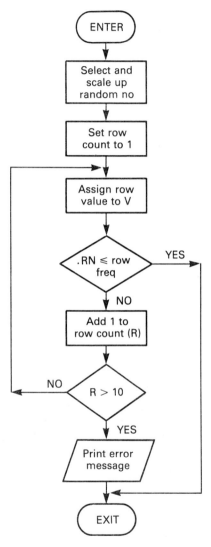

Fig. 9.1 Sampling flowchart

and the value of the scaled random number Z is compared with the current cumulative frequency (line 940). If Z is greater than the frequency the process is repeated for the next row (line 950). When, eventually, the random value Z falls within the current class interval the subroutine is left, carrying back the current value of the variable V. If, due to errors in setting up the distribution, the random value Z cannot be associated with any particular row then lines 960 and 970 are encountered, giving rise to the error message.

A stimulation program using this subroutine is given in Chapter 11, section 11.5.

Problem 3 – Input subroutine
Write a subroutine to allow the details of Table 9.10 to be entered into a two-dimensional array D. Make provision for up to ten rows to be entered.

A subroutine to meet the above requirements is shown in Table A12 (page 153).

10

Sound

10.1 Introduction to sound

Your computer has a 'music macro language' to make the sound facilities easy to implement. The concept is similar to the DRAW statement discussed in Chapter 7, where the equivalent sound command is PLAY. This chapter presents some programs that illustrate the features of the PLAY statement, such as changing notes and some programs that demonstrate their application, such as a siren and a traditional tune.

In addition to demonstrating the PLAY macro language this chapter also includes a program that demonstrates the use of the SOUND statement.

10.2 Macro sound language

The macro sound language allows a sequence of sound commands to be contained in a string or string variable. The string is used to define the sound parameters and note sequence when the PLAY statement is executed.

The following commands can be used in a PLAY string:

A to G Plays the indicated note in the current octave. A # or + sign after the note indicates a sharp, a − (minus) indicates a flat. Only normal sharps and flats are allowed (e.g. E# is invalid).

O *n* Sets the octave for the following notes. There are six octaves (i.e. *n* = 1 to 6). The default value of *n* is 4.

N *n* Plays note value *n*. This is an alternative way of specifying

the note. *n* can range from 0 to 84 (*n* = 0 means rest) where
fourth octave C is *n* = 49.

L *n* Sets the length of the following notes. The note length is 1/*n*
where *n* may range from 1 to 64. The default value of *n* is 4, i.e.
the note is 1/4 (a quarter note). If the value of *n* is put after a
note, without the L, the length applies only to that note (e.g.
E16 = L16E).

P *n* Sets a rest (pause) period where *n* is used as for the L
command.

A . after a note or a pause increases its length by a half. Several .
may be used in succession.

T *n* Sets the number of quarter notes per minute. *n* may range
from 32 to 255 and has a default value of 120.

M MS Plays the notes short with a pause between each, i.e.
staccato fashion.

ML Plays the notes smoothly with no pause between them,
i.e. legato fashion.

MN Plays the notes normally, i.e. not ML or MS.

In all the commands *n* can be specified directly or it can be a
variable. For example:

    PLAY"C"
or PLAY"N49"
or I = 49
    PLAY"N = I;"

will all play fourth octave C. Note that an equals sign and a
semi-colon are required within the string when *n* is specified as a
variable. It is also possible to build all the commands into a string
variable and execute it with an X command as follows:

    F$ = "CDEFGABO5C
    PLAY"XF$;"

In this example, F$ contain macro commands for a scale, C to C.
Note that the octave is changed (O5) for the final C. The use of X in
the PLAY statement causes the string F$ to be executed. A
semi-colon should follow any string used in this manner.

10.3 Note values

Table 10.1 Demonstration of full range of notes

```
10 CLS
20 FOR I=1 TO 84
30    LOCATE 10,30
40    PRINT "NOTE NO";I
50    PLAY "N = I;"
60 NEXT I
```

This program demonstrates the available range of notes and their associated numeric value. Line 50 plays the note using the default setting of a quarter note for length. Adding the following line will cause the notes to become shorter as the loop progresses,

45 PLAY "L = I;"

As L cannot exceed 64 the program will terminate with an execution error when the loop causes I to reach 65.

10.4 Tempo

Table 10.2 Demonstration of different tempos

```
10 CLS
20 FOR I=1 TO 7
30    READ TEMPO$,NPM
40    LOCATE 10,30
50    PRINT "THIS TEMPO IS:"
60    LOCATE 12,22
70    PRINT TEMPO$;" =";NPM;" NOTES PER MINUTE
80    LOCATE 14,33
90    PRINT "STACCATO"
100   PLAY "MS T=NPM; O3 CDEFGAB O4 C P2"
110   LOCATE 14,33
120   PRINT "LEGATO   "
130   PLAY "ML T=NPM; O3 CDEFGAB O4 C P2"
140 NEXT I
150 DATA "LARGO",50,"ADAGIO",70,"ANDANTE",90
160 DATA "MODERATO",110,"ALLEGRO",130
170 DATA "VIVACE",150,"PRESTO",170
```

The program given in Table 10.2 plays an octave scale at different tempos and also demonstrates the effects of staccato and legato. Seven tempos are demonstrated that approximate to common musical tempos such as Allegro etc.

The seven tempos are demonstrated within the loop over lines 20 to 140. Line 30 READs the description of the tempo and the notes per minute into variables TEMPO$ and NPM respectively from the DATA statements over lines 150 to 170. The current tempo information is located and printed to the screen over lines 40 to 70. A scale is then PLAYed firstly in staccato, line 100, and then in legato at line 130.

The effect of changing from staccato to legato is more noticeable at the slower tempos.

10.5 Playing tunes

The macro language makes it easy to play tunes. Table 10.3 gives a program that plays Frère Jacques.

Table 10.3 Playing a tune

```
10 REM FRERE JACQUES
20 PLAY "T120"
30 PLAY "GABG"
40 PLAY "GABG"
50 PLAY "B O5 CD2"
60 PLAY "O4"
70 PLAY "B O5 CD2"
80 PLAY "L8 DEDC L4 O4 BG"
90 PLAY "O5"
100 PLAY "L8 DEDC L4 O4 BG"
110 PLAY "GDG2"
120 PLAY "GDG2"
```

Line 20 has been incorporated so that you can try changing the tempo. The default value of T has been used in Table 10.3. Line 30 PLAYs the first phrase, and line 40 repeats it. Line 50 PLAYs the next phrase. The fifth octave is set in line 50 and so line 60 resets to the fourth octave before line 70 repeats the phrase. Notice that the final note (lines 50 and 70) is sounded twice as long.

Line 80 plays a sequence of notes that involve a change of octave, so line 90 resets the octave before line 100 repeats the sequence. Finally the tune finishes with line 110 repeated in line 120.

This program illustrates the scope for grouping notes for PLAYing in a systematic manner. If PLAY strings are built up without any regard to the 'pattern' of the music then debugging becomes harder.

10.6   A siren routine

Table 10.4   Two-tone siren

```
10 FOR N =1 TO 10
20     PLAY "CE"
30 NEXT N
```

Programming sound effects is largely a question of experimenting with different combinations of notes, their durations and pauses. The program in Table 10.4 illustrates the use of the PLAY statement to produce a two-tone siren effect. The program simply repeatedly sounds two notes over and over again by means of the loop in lines 10 to 30.

10.7   A simulated phone ring

Table 10.5   Ringing phone program

```
10 PLAY "L64 O5"
20 FOR R=1 TO 8
30     FOR N=1 TO 2
40         FOR T=1 TO 12
50             PLAY "F"
60         NEXT T
70         PLAY "P8"
80     NEXT N
90     PLAY "P1"
100 NEXT R
```

The program in Table 10.5 simulates the ringing of a phone. The phone rings eight times, each ring consisting of two short 'trills'.

Line 10 sets the length and octave of the note to be PLAYed. The eight rings are simulated within the loop over lines 20 to 100. The two trills of each ring are sounded within the N loop (lines 30 to 80). A trill consists of note F (line 50), played twelve times within the T loop (lines 40 to 60). After one trill there is a short pause, due to line 70, before the second trill. Similarly there is a pause (line 90) between each ring.

This program illustrates how patterns of sound can be built up by nested FOR loops.

10.8 The SOUND statement

The general form of the sound statement is,

SOUND f,d

where

f = the pitch in hertz, from 37 to 32767
d = duration in 0.055 sec units, from 0 to 65535

The specified pitch does not have to be an integer value. Middle C which has a frequency of 523.25 can therefore be produced by the following statement,

SOUND 523.25,18

A duration value of 18 is approximately equivalent to one second.

Table 10.6   Demonstration of SOUND statement

```
10 CLS
20 FOR I=100 TO 10000 STEP 100
30    LOCATE 10,30
40    SOUND I,10
50    PRINT "FREQUENCY";I
60 NEXT I
```

The program in Table 10.6 illustrates the use of the SOUND statement by producing frequencies over the range 100 to 10000 in steps of 100. This program can provide a quick check on the user's upper audio range. If necessary the range for the loop variable, I, can be increased to 20000 to embrace the range covered by 'hi-fi' equipment.

Problem
Write a program to act as a timer alarm. The time duration should be entered in minutes and the screen should display the elapsed time in minutes and seconds. As the timing count proceeds a ticking noise should be heard. When the required elapsed time is reached an alarm is sounded. A suitable program is listed in Table A13 (page 153).

11

Range of Applications

11.1 Series

A series consists of a number of terms, each term having a constant relationship to the next term. When devising computer programs for evaluating series, a procedure needs to be designed which allows the next term in the series to be calculated from the previous term.

For example, the exponential series may be evaluated as follows:

$$e^x = 1 + x + \frac{x^2}{2!} + \frac{x^3}{3!} + \dots$$

where $2! = 1 \times 2$ $3! = 1 \times 2 \times 3$, etc.

The steps in the repetitive process to calculate e^x to n terms are:

Step 1   (initialisation), set first term (T) to x, e^x to $1 + T$, and I to 2
Step 2   calculate next term by multiplying previous term by x/I, and add this new term to the old value of e^x
Step 3   repeat step 2 a further $n - 2$ times.

The BASIC routine to calculate e^x is shown in Table 11.1.

Table 11.1   Program to calculate e^x

```
10 INPUT "NO OF TERMS FOR E^X";N
20 INPUT "VALUE OF X";X
30 T=X
40 E=1+T
50 FOR I=2 TO N
60    T=T*X/I
70    E=E+T
80 NEXT I
90 PRINT
100 PRINT "E^";X;"=";E
110 PRINT "**********************"
```

Problem 1 – Evaluation of cos *x*

Write a BASIC program for evaluating cos *x*, given that:

$$\cos x = 1 - \frac{x^2}{2!} + \frac{x^4}{4!} - \frac{x^6}{6!} + \dots$$

The program is listed in Table A14 (page 154).

11.2 Processing experimental data

Table 11.2 'Heat of combustion' problem

```
10 CLS
20 PRINT "HEAT OF COMBUSTION"
30 PRINT "--------------------"
40 PRINT
50 INPUT "NAME OF SUBSTANCE";N$
60 INPUT "ENTER S,W,T,R";S,W,T,R
70 H=INT(W*4.2*T*R*.001/S+.5)
80 PRINT
90 PRINT "RESULT FOR ";N$;" = ";H;" KJ/MOL"
100 PRINT "*************************************"
110 PRINT
120 INPUT "ANY MORE DATA (Y=YES,N=NO)";Y$
130 PRINT
140 IF Y$ = "Y" THEN 40
```

The program given in Table 11.2 illustrates the use of the computer to process data which is entered at run time from the keyboard in response to messages output from the program. This method of working is applicable to, say, a class of students where each group is carrying out similar experiments. The results of the experiments are prepared for input to the computer program, and the program is used to output the final answer for each group. Similarly, a scientist may repeat the same experiments for different substances and the series of results may then be processed by one computer program.

The output messages, replies (data input) and results are shown in Table 11.3. S is the mass of substance burnt and W the mass of water heated by the substance in grammes, T is the rise in temperature of the water in °C, and R is the relative molecular mass.

Table 11.3   Output from Table 11.2 and data input

```
HEAT OF COMBUSTION
------------------------------------
NAME OF SUBSTANCE? ETHANOL
ENTER S,W,T,R? .36,100,23.5,46
RESULT FOR ETHANOL = 1261 KJ/MOL
*****************************************
ANY MORE DATA (Y = YES, N = NO)?Y
NAME OF SUBSTANCE? METHANOL
ENTER S,W,T,R? .39,99,21.2,32
RESULT FOR METHANOL = 723 KJ/MOL
*****************************************
ANY MORE DATA (Y = YES, N = NO)?Y
NAME OF SUBSTANCE? PROPANOL
ENTER S,W,T,R? .31,101,24.8,60
RESULT FOR PROPANOL = 2036 KJ/MOL
*****************************************
ANY MORE DATA (Y = YES, N = NO)?N
```

Problem 2 – Roots of quadratic equations

Write a program to calculate the values of the roots of any number of quadratic equations ($ax^2 + bx + c = 0$), given the coefficients a, b and c. If $b^2 - 4ac > 0$, output the message 'REAL ROOTS' and the two roots. If $b^2 - 4ac = 0$, output the message 'COINCIDENT ROOTS', and the value $= -b/2a$. If $b^2 - 4ac < 0$, output the message 'COMPLEX ROOTS'. Allow for interactive entry of a, b and c during run time and stop the execution of the program by zeros being entered for a, b and c. The program is listed in Table A15 (page 154), and the answers for the equations shown in Table 11.4 are given in Appendix B (page 159).

Table 11.4   Quadratic equations

$$3x^2 + 9x + 2 = 0$$
$$7x^2 - 5x + 3 = 0$$
$$x^2 - 8x + 16 = 0$$
$$2x^2 + 3x - 4 = 0$$
$$-3x^2 - 2x + 1 = 0$$
$$x^2 + 2x + 3 = 0$$
$$4x^2 + 4x + 1 = 0$$

11.3 Tabulation of results and averaging

Measurements, intermediate calculations and final results of experiments may need to be tabulated so that a permanent record is available in an easily readable form. The final answer is often obtained by averaging the results of more than one experiment.

Problem 3 – Width of a slit

The collimator of a spectrometer was used to provide a parallel beam of light from a sodium flame. The beam of light was allowed to fall on a slit placed vertically at the centre of the table of the spectrometer. When appropriate adjustments had been made, parallel bands were seen on looking through the telescope. These were made as sharp as possible by adjusting the slit of the collimator. The crosswires of the eyepiece of the telescope were set on corresponding minima on either side of the centre and the vernier readings were noted; this gave a value of 2A for each of the fringes 1 to 6.

Table 11.5 Tabulation of results for Problem 3

FRINGE NUMBER	VERNIER DEG	MIN	READINGS DEG	MIN	A MIN	WIDTH OF SLIT CM
1	41	26	41	20	3	.0675
	221	25	221	19		
2	41	29	41	17		
	221	27	221	15		
3	41	33	41	15		
	221	31	221	13		
4	41	35	41	11		
	221	34	221	10		
5	41	39	41	9		
	221	38	221	8		
6	41	41	41	5		
	221	40	221	4		

The width of the slit W (cm) = Nλ/A where N is the fringe number, λ = 5.893 × 10^{-5} cm (wavelength of sodium light), and A is in radians.

Write a program to tabulate the measurements taken and values of A and W as shown in Table 11.5, and output the average value of the width of the slit. There are two pairs of vernier readings for each fringe number. Values of 2A are found by subtracting the second vernier reading from the first vernier reading. The average value of A is then calculated for each fringe number. The program is listed in Table A16 (page 155), and the average value of W is given in Appendix B (page 159).

11.4 Linear regression

Often straight line graphs may be obtained by manipulating the formula which defines the relationship between the variables. The equation of a straight line may be written as,

$$y = mx + c$$

where
   x = the independent variable
   y = the dependent variable
   m = the slope of the line
   c = the intercept of the line on the y axis

A line of 'best fit' can be calculated for a series of data points from,

$$m = \frac{n\Sigma xy - \Sigma x\Sigma y}{n\Sigma x^2 - (\Sigma x)^2}$$

and
$$c = \frac{\Sigma y - m\Sigma x}{n}$$

where
   x and y are the coordinates of each data point and
   n = number of data points.

There are many equivalent forms of the above expression; some are more suited to manual calculation than programming. A measure of how closely the data follows the calculated straight line is given by the coefficient of correlation (r). If the data lies on a perfectly straight line then *r* will be +1 (for positive slope) or −1 (for negative slope). In the extreme case of no correlation whatsoever (i.e. the points are scattered randomly) *r* will equal zero. The acceptable level of correlation (i.e. value of *r*) for the number of readings involved can be found from statistical tables.

Again, the formulae for *r* can be presented in different ways. The expression given below is in a convenient form for programming when the slope is already evaluated.

$$r = \sqrt{\frac{m(\Sigma xy - \Sigma x \Sigma y/n)}{\Sigma y^2 - (\Sigma y)^2/n}}$$

It should be noted that *m*, *c* and *r* require similarly preliminary calculations and that it is convenient to calculate initially and store,

$$\Sigma x, \Sigma y, \Sigma x^2, \Sigma y^2, \Sigma x \Sigma y$$

Table 11.6 Linear regression routine

```
10 CLS
20 DIM X(20),Y(20)
30 INPUT "ENTER NO OF PAIRS OF READINGS";N
40 FOR I=1 TO N
50    INPUT "ENTER X,Y PAIR ";X(I),Y(I)
60 NEXT I
70 GOSUB 4000
80 END
4000 S1=0
4010 S2=0
4020 S3=0
4030 S4=0
4040 S5=0
4050 FOR I=1 TO N
4060     S1=S1+X(I)
4070     S2=S2+Y(I)
4080     S3=S3+X(I)^2
4090     S4=S4+Y(I)^2
4100     S5=S5+X(I)*Y(I)
4110 NEXT I
4120 M=(N*S5-S2*S1)/(N*S3-S1^2)
4130 C=(S2-M*S1)/N
4140 R=(M*(S5-S1*S2/N))/(S4-S2^2/N)
4150 PRINT
4160 PRINT "Y = M*X+C"
4170 PRINT "M =";M
4180 PRINT "C =";C
4190 PRINT
4200 PRINT "COEFF. OF CORRELATION =";SQR(R)
4210 RETURN
```

A program to perform linear regression and calculate *r* is given in Table 11.6.

Problem 4 – Young's modulus of the material of a bar

The bar was clamped horizontally at one end. A weight of mass M (kg) was attached to the other end, and was kept vibrating by an electro-magnet. The vibrating end of the bar was illuminated and was viewed through a slit in a rotating disc, using a telescope. The speed of the disc was gradually increased by adjusting the resistance, placed in series with the electric motor used to rotate the disc, until the bar appeared to be at rest when it was vibrating. A counting arrangement on the motor gave the number of rotations in a definite time.

It can be shown that the motion of the vibrating bar is simple harmonic with a period:

$$T = 2\pi \sqrt{\left(\frac{l^3(M + 33/140m)}{3Yi} \right)}$$

where

i is the moment of inertia of cross-section
Y is Young's modulus of the material of the bar
l is the length of the bar in metres
m is the mass in kg of the vibrating part of the bar

For a bar of rectangular cross-section (breadth b and depth d metres), $i = bd^3/12$.

Hence
$$\frac{3Ybd^3T^2}{48\pi^2 l^3} = M + 33/140m$$

T^2 (seconds) plotted for different values of M (kg) gives a straight line graph, and Y may be found using the slope of the graph as follows:

$$Y = \frac{1}{\text{slope of graph}} \frac{16\pi^2 l^3}{bd^3}$$

Write a program to output Young's modulus for a bar in Newtons/m^2. Use the linear regression routine given in Table 11.6, to find the slope of the graph for the values of T and M given in Table 11.7. The dimensions of the bar are: $b = 1.58\,cm$, $d = 0.312\,cm$, $l = 40\,cm$. The results are given in Appendix B (page 160).

Note: Remember to calculate T^2 for the linear regression 'Y' values; the 'X' values are those listed under M.

Table 11.7 Data for Problem 4

M *(kg)*	T *(seconds)*
.097	0.12
.147	0.139
.157	0.145
.177	0.15
.197	0.16

11.5 Simulation

11.5.1 Background

Simulation requires the writing of a program that models a situation. Changes are brought about in the model, either by the user or by inbuilt routines so that the behaviour of the model can be studied. From studying the behaviour of the model under varying circumstances it is hoped to gain a better understanding of the reality represented by the model.

Some models consist of specific relationships (e.g. a Balance Sheet). In such a case, if you make a change in one variable this leads to a specific revised Balance Sheet. You can, by this means, simulate the effect of changes in labour costs on the profits.

Many forms of simulation require the values of some of the variables to be sampled from a probable range of values. The probable range of values is usually expressed as a probability (or frequency) distribution. In these models, the outcomes and their interactions need to be studied over many simulations to obtain a representative picture of the model's behaviour.

A simple simulation model of this type is discussed below. As the basis of the variability is the sampling from a frequency distribution, the program has been written to make use of the two subroutines previously developed in Chapter 9, section 9.6. Note how the subroutine can be used several times by transferring values to and from the variables common to the subroutine.

11.5.2 Simulation of combined units

The problem is to simulate the breakdown pattern of a combined unit comprising a motor assembly and a gear assembly from the breakdown pattern of the individual assemblies.

The running time of a combined unit can be simulated by sampling in turn from the running time distributions of the motor unit and the gear unit. The shorter running time will be the running time of the combined unit. By simulating many such samples the MTBF (mean time between failure) for a combined unit can be obtained.

11.5.3 Output required

For a short simulation it is convenient to monitor the course of each pass through the program. Therefore, in this case, the output can be the sampled lives of the motor and gear assemblies, the life of the combined unit and the MTBF to date. For longer simulations this amount of detail would be time consuming to print. It could be incorporated for debugging purposes and then dropped, the final program only producing the ultimate MTBF.

However, a single final statement of the value of the MTBF is not as informative as a running output of the variable. The decision to terminate a simulation is often taken once the variable under inspection has settled down. These considerations, in this case, lead to the idea that there should be an option to continue the run if the fluctuation in the MTBF is not within the desired limits.

11.5.4 Description of the program

The BASIC listing of the main routine is shown in Table 11.8, and of the subroutines in Tables 9.12 and A12 (see Chapter 9).

Table 11.8a   Main routine for simulation program

```
5 CLS
10 DIM M(10,2),G(10,2),D(10,2),X(10,2)
20 GOSUB 800
30 FOR I=1 TO N
40    M(I,1)=D(I,1)
50    M(I,2)=D(I,2)
60 NEXT I
70 GOSUB 800
80 FOR I=1 TO N
90    G(I,1)=D(I,1)
100   G(I,2)=D(I,2)
```

```
110 NEXT I
120 U$="----------------------------------------"
130 T=0
140 K=1
150 PRINT
160 INPUT "LENGTH OF SIMULATION";L
170 PRINT
180 PRINT U$
190 PRINT "SIM";TAB(6);"MOTOR";TAB(14);"GEAR";
200 PRINT TAB(22);"COMB.";TAB(30);"MTBF"
210 PRINT U$.
220 FOR S=K TO L
230     FOR I=1 TO 10
240         X(I,1)=M(I,1)
250         X(I,2)=M(I,2)
260     NEXT I
270     GOSUB 900
280     U1=V
290     FOR I=1 TO 10
300         X(I,1)=G(I,1)
310         X(I,2)=G(I,2)
320     NEXT I
```

The motor unit frequency distribution is input after control is transferred to the subroutine from line 20. The input is returned in array D and the contents copied to array M. This allows array D and hence the subroutine to be used again. This time the gear unit frequency distribution is input and on return to the main routine it is copied from array D to array G.

The next stage of the program initialises the variables T and K in readiness for the simulation. Variable T is the cumulative combined unit running time, and variable K is the starting (or continuation) value of the simulation count. K is initially set at one for the first run (line 140) and is revised in line 440 in case the FOR loop is to be continued.

The initial length of the simulation is input at line 160. Lines 190 and 200 print the required heading. PRINT U$ produces a line of dashes and is used to highlight the headings (lines 180 and 210). Each line of calculated output is produced within the FOR loop from lines 220 to 420.

Table 11.8b Main routine for simulation program (cont.)

```
330     GOSUB 900
340     U2=V
350     C=U1
360     IF U2 > U1 THEN 380
```

```
370    C=U2
380    T=T+C
390    A=T/S
400    A=INT(10*A)/10
410    PRINT S;TAB(6);U1;TAB(14);U2;TAB(22);C;TAB(30);A
420 NEXT S
430 PRINT U$
440 K=L+1
450 PRINT "ENTER ADDITIONAL SIMULATIONS"
460 PRINT "REQUIRED, OR ZERO TO STOP";
470 INPUT L
480 IF L > 0 THEN 500
490 END
500 L=K+L-1
510 GOTO 210
```

Table 11.9   Example of output from Table 11.8

INPUT LENGTH OF SIMULATION ? 10

SIM	MOTOR	GEAR	COMB.	MTBF
1	16	18	16	16
2	16	14	14	15
3	8	16	8	12.6
4	16	18	16	13.5
5	16	14	14	13.6
6	8	14	8	12.6
7	12	22	12	12.5
8	20	22	20	13.5
9	16	10	10	13.1
10	4	14	4	12.1

ENTER ADDITIONAL SIMULATIONS
REQUIRED, OR ZERO TO STOP ? 5

SIM	MOTOR	GEAR	COMB.	MTBF
11	16	14	14	12.3
12	12	14	12	12.3
13	16	18	16	12.6
14	16	16	16	12.8
15	12	18	12	12.8

ENTER ADDITIONAL SIMULATIONS
REQUIRED, OR ZERO TO STOP ? 0

To sample from the motor unit distribution (array M) it is copied to array X by lines 230 to 260. The subroutine starting at line 900 is entered and a sample from array X is returned as variable V. In line 280 this value is retained for future reference as variable U1. This procedure is then repeated for the gear unit, the sampled value being retained as U2. Lines 350 to 370 carry forward the lower of the two values as variable C (this is the running time of the combined unit). The cumulative running time is calculated in line 380 and the current average running time (the MTBF) is calculated in line 390 as A. Having completed a pass through the FOR loop, a line of output provides the current simulated values of U1, U2, C and A.

After simulating the stipulated number of times (i.e. L), the FOR loop is left. In anticipation of continuing, the value of K is reset in line 440. Lines 450 to 470 allow you to reset L, or, if you enter zero, the run stops.

To separate this interactive part of the run from the previously calculated output, PRINT U$ is now used in line 430. If the run is to be continued, control is returned to line 210 to separate the subsequent output in a similar way. This means of trying to keep the output tidy is best appreciated by studying extracts from a run of this program as shown in Table 11.9.

Problem 5 – Combined units simulation
Use the simulation program (Table 11.8) to calculate the mean time between failure for a combined unit consisting of motor and gear units having the failure pattern shown in Table 11.10. Simulate 100 failures. The answer is given in Appendix B (page 160).

Table 11.10 Failure pattern of units

Motor Unit		Gear Unit	
Life (weeks)	*Cum % Freq*	*Life (weeks)*	*Cum % Freq*
4	20	10	10
8	40	12	15
12	50	14	40
16	90	16	60
20	100	18	75
		20	80
		22	100

11.6 Financial

Many financial calculations relate to the calculation of interest over a period of time. A common example involving repayment of interest (and capital) is a mortgage repayment. Once a mortgage has been obtained there is little you can do about the repayments required. A computer program, however, could be particularly useful in examining the effects of changing the variables to assist in choosing the most suitable mortgage.

11.6.1 Mortgage calculations

The repayments required on a mortgage can be calculated from the following formula:

$$R = \frac{Pi(1 + i)^n}{(1 + i)^n - 1}$$

where

P = Principal (the amount borrowed)
n = duration of mortgage
i = interest rate per annum
R = required annual repayment

Many organisations providing mortgages allow you to repay monthly. The monthly repayments are usually $\frac{1}{12}$ of the annual repayments because they are regarded as simply advance payments of the annual premium. These monthly advance payments do not themselves earn interest.

11.6.2 Requirements of the program

In examining alternative mortgage proposals you would want to change P, n and/or i as required. As successive changes were made it would be useful to be reminded as to the current values of these three variables.

This program is the type likely to be used by someone such as a broker in a working environment. As he is not likely to have any programming knowledge the PRINT messages need to be clear and the data entered in the most natural way. Thus the variables to be revised are indicated by entering i, P or n rather than entering a numeric alternative such as 1, 2 or 3. Although the program is slightly more complex as a result, this is regarded as a secondary consideration.

The input to the program is straightforward; the interest rate is entered as a percentage (i.e. 12.5 not .125) as this is how it is commonly quoted.

11.6.3 Description of the program

A listing of the program is given in Table 11.11 and an example of the output in Table 11.12.

Table 11.11 Program for mortgage calculation

```
10 REM MORTGAGE REPAYMENT
15 CLS
20 DEF FNM(X)=INT(X*100+.5)/100
30 INPUT "ENTER INTEREST RATE AS A %";I
40 I=I/100
50 INPUT "ENTER SIZE OF MORTGAGE";P
60 INPUT "ENTER PERIOD OF LOAN (YRS)";N
70 R=(P*I*(1+I)^N)/(((1+I)^N)-1)
80 PRINT "MONTHLY REPAYMENTS =";
90 PRINT FNM(R/12)
100 PRINT
110 PRINT "ENTER I,P OR N TO REVISE"
120 PRINT "INTEREST, PRINCIPAL OR YEARS"
130 PRINT:PRINT "EXISTING VALUES ARE"
140 PRINT I;P;N
150 PRINT:PRINT "OR ENTER S TO STOP"
160 INPUT A$
170 IF A$="S" THEN END
180 INPUT "ENTER REVISED VALUE";X
190 IF A$="I" THEN 250
200 IF A$="P" THEN 260
210 IF A$="N" THEN 270
220 PRINT:PRINT "REVISION ERROR: ";
230 PRINT A$;" ENTERED":PRINT
240 GOTO 110
250 I=X/100:GOTO 70
260 P=X:GOTO 70
270 N=X:GOTO 70
```

Line 20 defines the function FNM which rounds to two decimal places thereby representing monetary amounts to the nearest penny. Lines 30 to 60 request the starting values of I, P and N. The annual repayment is calculated in line 70 and printed as a monthly repayment in line 90. A blank line (line 100) is printed before looping and producing revised output.

Table 11.12   Example of output from Table 11.11

```
ENTER INTEREST RATE AS A % ? 12.5
ENTER SIZE OF MORTGAGE ? 10000
ENTER PERIOD OF LOAN (YRS) ? 25
MONTHLY REPAYMENTS = 109.95

ENTER I,P OR N TO REVISE
INTEREST, PRINCIPAL OR YEARS
EXISTING VALUES ARE
.125    10000    25
OR ENTER S TO STOP
? P
ENTER REVISED VALUE ? 8000
MONTHLY REPAYMENTS = 87.96

ENTER I,P OR N TO REVISE
INTEREST, PRINCIPAL OR YEARS
EXISTING VALUES ARE
.125    8000    25
OR ENTER S TO STOP
? S
```

Line 160 allows you to revise optionally the values of I, P or N (line 140 reminds you of the current values). The option you enter is identified by the program over lines 170 to 210. If an inappropriate character is entered, this character 'falls through' these lines and the error message (lines 220–230) is printed. Otherwise the revised value entered in line 180 is assigned accordingy over lines 250 to 270. The program then loops back to line 70 to recalculate R.

Problem 6 – Monthly repayments
Run the program shown in Table 11.11 using the following data:

Interest rate, 11%; Loan, £15,000; Period of loan, 20 years

Then revise the loan to £20,000. The two monthly repayments are given in Appendix B (page 160).

12

Using a Printer and Disk Unit

12.1 Printers

Two main types of printer that are used with microcomputers are matrix printers and daisy-wheel printers. Matrix printers print each character as a grid of dots, while daisy-wheel printers have the character set embossed on the circumference of the print-wheel. The latter is interchangeable so that different character sets and type founts can be used. Daisy-wheel printers tend to be more expensive than matrix printers and are used for 'letter-quality' printing.

Matrix printers have a standard character set built into the printer, but special characters can be programmed such as graphics characters. Many printers have a set of switches that allow a range of character sets to be used. The hash symbol (#) is part of the American character set. When the switches are set to the UK character set a pound symbol (£) is produced instead of the hash. As the precise details vary from printer to printer, it is important to consult the appropriate printer manual.

```
This is NORMAL size printing
DOUBLE  WIDTH  mode
The printer reverts back at next line
CHR$(15) converts to CONDENSED mode
This mode remains in force until changed
CHR$(18) converts to NORMAL mode
```

Fig. 12.1   Output from printer control program (*see Table 12.2*)

12.2   Output to the printer from a program

A program which outputs to the printer is shown in Tables 12.1a and
12.1b. This is an enhanced version of the simple program given in
Table 2.2 (page 10), and gives the user a choice of printing letter
headings, notebook labels or envelope labels. The enhancements
include:

A menu of options	(lines 70–150)
Variable parameters	(lines 220–250,
for each option	420–430, 720)
Centering the name in	(lines 460–640)
a border of asterisks	

Table 12.1a   Enhanced name and address program

```
10 SCREEN 0,0:CLS:PRINT
20 LINE INPUT "TITLE            :";T$:PRINT
30 LINE INPUT "NAME            :";N$:PRINT
40 LINE INPUT "1ST ADDRESS LINE :";A$:PRINT
50 LINE INPUT "2ND ADDRESS LINE :";B$:PRINT
60 LINE INPUT "3RD ADDRESS LINE :";C$
70 CLS:PRINT "    SELECT OPTION"
80 PRINT "    ------------"
90 PRINT:PRINT
100 PRINT "1  LETTER HEADING"       -
110 PRINT:PRINT "2  NOTEBOOK LABELS"
120 PRINT:PRINT "3  ENVELOPE LABELS"
130 PRINT:PRINT "4  END OF PROGRAM"
140 PRINT:PRINT:PRINT
150 INPUT "OPTION";C
160 ON C GOSUB 200,400,700,900
170 GOTO 70
200 REM LETTER HEADING
210 CLS:PRINT
220 INPUT "NUMBER OF SHEETS";N:PRINT
230 INPUT "PAGE LENGTH";P:PRINT
240 INPUT "TOP MARGIN";T:PRINT
250 INPUT "START POSITION";S
260 OPEN "LPT1:" FOR OUTPUT AS #1
270 FOR I=1 TO N
280     FOR J=1 TO T
290         PRINT #1," "
300     NEXT J
310     PRINT #1,TAB(S);A$
320     PRINT #1,TAB(S);B$
330     PRINT #1,TAB(S);C$
340     FOR J=1 TO P-T-3
350         PRINT #1," "
```

```
360      NEXT J
370 NEXT I
380 CLOSE 1
390 RETURN
```

Table 12.1b Enhanced name and address program (cont.)

```
400 REM NOTEBOOK LABELS
410 CLS:PRINT
420 INPUT "NUMBER OF LABELS";N:PRINT
430 INPUT "START POSITION";S
440 OPEN "LPT1:" FOR OUTPUT AS #1
450 L=LEN(N$)
460 FOR I=1 TO N
470      PRINT #1,TAB(S);"***********************"
480      PRINT #1,TAB(S);"*                     *"
490      PRINT #1,TAB(S);"*                     *"
500      SP=INT((20-L)/2)
510      PRINT #1,TAB(S);"*";
520      FOR K=1 TO SP
530           PRINT #1," ";
540      NEXT K
550      PRINT #1,N$
560      FOR K=1 TO 20-L-SP
570           PRINT #1," ";
580      NEXT K
590      PRINT #1,"*"
600      PRINT #1,TAB(S);"*                     *"
610      PRINT #1,TAB(S);"*                     *"
620      PRINT #1,TAB(S);"***********************"
630      PRINT #1," ":PRINT #1," ":PRINT #1," "
640 NEXT I
650 CLOSE 1
660 RETURN
700 REM ENVELOPE LABELS
710 CLS:PRINT
720 INPUT "TOTAL NUMBER OF LABELS(EVEN)";N
730 OPEN "LPT1:" FOR OUTPUT AS #1
740 FOR I=1 TO N/2
750      PRINT #1,TAB(10);T$;" ";N$;
760      PRINT #1,SPC(34-LEN(N$+T$));T$;" ";N$
770      PRINT #1,TAB(10);A$;SPC(35-LEN(A$));A$
780      PRINT #1,TAB(10);B$;SPC(35-LEN(B$));B$
790      PRINT #1,TAB(10);C$;SPC(35-LEN(C$));C$
800      PRINT #1," ":PRINT #1," ":PRINT #1," "
810 NEXT I
820 CLOSE 1
830 RETURN
900 END
```

The output to the printer is achieved by specifying PRINT #1 as the print command, having opened file 1 to the printer (LPT1:) in lines 260, 440 and 730. At the end of each print option, file 1 is closed (lines 380, 650 and 820).

Note output to the screen is by means of ordinary PRINT statements (for example, lines 70–130). The LINE INPUT and INPUT messages also appear on the screen (for example, lines 20–60 and line 150).

When outputting to the printer, you should use a SPC (space) function instead of TAB, after the first TAB in a print statement. When using SPC, it is important that the number of spaces moved takes into account the length of any previously printed output on that line. One way of achieving this is shown in line 770, in which SPC(35-LEN(A$)) 'spaces' from the end of A$ to the thirty-fifth print position from the start of A$.

A new statement has been introduced in line 160, the ON . . . GOSUB statement. This works in a similar way to the ON . . . GOTO statement discussed in Chapter 5, but branches to *subroutines* according to the value of the expression or variable after the word ON (that is, C in the example in line 160).

Line 160 causes a branch to line 200, 400, 700 or 900 depending on whether 1, 2, 3 or 4 has been entered in response to line 150 for variable C. For example, if 1 is entered from the keyboard in response to OPTION? (line 150), then a branch will be made to line 200 and lines 210 to 380 will be executed. When line 390 (RETURN) is reached the program will branch to the line following the ON . . . GOSUB statement, that is, line 170 which branches back to line 70 to select the next option. To end the program run, 4 is entered as the option and a branch is made to 900 (END), so no RETURN statement is required.

For some applications, you may want to give a choice of outputting to the screen *or* to the printer. This may be done with the subroutine given below, which is used for the file processing and reporting example in Chapter 14. The subroutine sets a string variable A$ to "SCRN:" or "LPT1:" depending on whether an S (for output to the screen) or a P (for output to the printer) is entered in response to the INPUT statement in line 7820.

```
7800 REM SET UP OUTPUT DEVICE
7810 PRINT
7820 INPUT "OUTPUT TO SCREEN OR PRINTER,
S/P";B$
7830 IF B$ = "S" THEN A$ = "SCRN:"
7840 IF B$ = "P" THEN A$ = "LPT1:"
7850 IF B$ < > "S" AND B$ < > "P" THEN 7820
7860 RETURN
```

A$ can then be used in an OPEN statement to output to the screen or printer, for example:

```
4530 OPEN A$ FOR OUTPUT AS #1
```

The AND used in line 7850 is termed a *logical operator*. In this case the THEN part of the line will be executed only if both tests on B$ are true. Another logical operator is OR. In this case the THEN part of the line will be executed if any of the relationships are true.

Not all BASICs use SCRN: or LPT1: for the screen and printer device names. You should check your manuals to find the names appropriate to the version of BASIC you are using.

12.3   Controlling a printer

Modern dot matrix printers usually offer a range of printing styles. When the printer is powered up it sets itself to its 'normal' mode. Other modes may include italic, condensed, double width etc. Although many of the printer's options can be set by switches built into the printer it is also usually possible to control these settings via instructions within BASIC programs. This is done by sending appropriate character codes to the printer using a PRINT statement. The program shown in Table 12.2 illustrates how this is done.

Table 12.2   Demonstration of printer control (*reduced size*)

```
10 REM DEMO OF SOME PRINTER FONT SIZES
20 LPRINT "This is NORMAL size printing"
30 LPRINT CHR$(14);"DOUBLE WIDTH mode"
40 LPRINT "The printer reverts back at next line"
50 LPRINT CHR$(15);"CHR$(15) converts to CONDENSED mode"
60 LPRINT"This mode remains in force until changed"
70 LPRINT CHR$(18);"CHR$(18) converts to NORMAL mode"
```

Lines 20 to 70 make use of the LPRINT form of the print statement, previously mentioned in Chapter 2. Line 20 prints a line of text representing the normal power up mode. This is usually 10 characters per inch. Line 30 then converts the printing mode to double width characters. This is achieved by sending the appropriate value (usually 14) as a CHR$ code. Double width mode usually only persists for the line being printed. Line 40 demonstrates that the printer has reverted to normal mode. Line 50 sends the value 15 to convert the printer into condensed mode. This mode usually persists and so line 60 should also be printed in condensed mode. Sending the value of 18 in line 70 converts the printer back to normal mode. (The output from the program is shown on page 111.)

The manual supplied with your printer will contain a list of all the codes that can be used from a program. The more sophisticated printers allow superscripts and subscripts to be printed, underlining to be introduced, line spacing to be changed and various page settings to be altered. The program in Table 12.2 can be readily edited or extended to try out the effects of other code values.

12.4   Disk commands

A range of commands exist for communicating with a disk drive and processing disk-based programs. Some, such as LOAD and SAVE are directly related to processing disk-based BASIC programs, others relate to manipulating the programs or files on the disk (for example, NAME) while within BASIC. In addition to this there are a range of disk operating system (DOS) commands available outside of BASIC.

The DOS commands are independent of BASIC and can vary according to the computer. The two most widely used disk operating systems are MSDOS[1] (and variations such as PCDOS[2]) and CP/M[3]. With some microcomputers you have the choice of which to use. The range of commands available in a DOS include:

a format command to set up a new disk;
a directory command to list the files on the disk;

[1] MSDOS is a trademark of Microsoft
[2] PCDOS is a trademark of IBM
[3] CP/M is a trademark of Digital Research

an erase command to delete files from the disk;
a rename command to change the name of files;
a copy command to copy files between disks.

Further details of these commands will be found in the manuals supplied with your computer. The following section deals with the disk commands that are available within BASIC. These commands could vary between different versions of BASIC but there should be an equivalent available in most BASICs.

FILE NAMES

File names consist of two parts, a name of up to 8 characters and an optional extension of at most 3 characters. The extension is preceded by a period (.), e.g.

SALES.JAN

Two characters, ? and * can be used as wild cards when specifying file names. The ? is used to denote the specific position of any character, e.g.

SALES.J?N

would encompass

SALES.JAN
SALES.JUN

The * is used to represent any string of one or more ? characters, e.g.

SALES.*

would cncompass

SALES.JAN
SALES.FEB
SALES.MAR
etc.

From this it follows that *.* encompasses every file name.

FILES

The FILES command is used within BASIC to list appropriate files from the current disk onto the screen. Using the command as,

    FILES

or

    FILES "*.*"

will list all the files from the disk. A subset of the files can be listed by using the wild card characters as previously described.

LOAD, SAVE and RUN

Once BASIC has been invoked a BASIC program stored as a file on a disk can be transferred into the computer's memory by the following command:

    LOAD *"program name"*

If the disk is not in the default drive the program name is preceded by the drive specifier. For example, if the default drive is A and the program disk is in drive B the command becomes:

    LOAD *"B:program name"*

Once the program has been LOADed the command RUN will cause the program to be executed.

A similar command format is used to SAVE a BASIC program as a disk file, i.e.

    SAVE *"B:program name"*

This command would SAVE the program to drive unit B.

If a file name extension is not given, BASIC file names have an extension of .BAS automatically added when the SAVE command is used, e.g.

    SAVE "MYPROG"

would result in the file saved to disk having the name,

    MYPROG.BAS

It is not necessary to specify the .BAS extension with the LOAD command, e.g.

    LOAD "MYPROG"

is sufficient.

NAME
The NAME command is used to change the name of a file, its format is,

NAME "*program name*" AS "*program name*"

e.g.

NAME "MEMO.JAN" AS "NOTE-1.JAN"

When using the NAME command the full file name including extensions, if any, must be given.

KILL
The KILL command is used to erase the specified files from the disk. Wild cards can be used with this command for some versions of BASIC. If wild cards are to be used it is advisable to first use the proposed wild card format in a FILES command to check which files would be acted on. For example,

KILL "SALES.*"

will erase all "SALES" files from the disk.

MERGE
This command allows a program on the disk to be merged with the program currently in memory. The program to be merged from the disk must have been SAVEd in ASCII format by using a special form of the SAVE command. For example, to SAVE a program, PROG2, in ASCII format use the command:

SAVE "PROG2",A

If a program, PROG1, is currently loaded into memory then the program PROG2 can now be merged by:

MERGE "PROG2"

If the two programs have any line numbers in common then the lines from the incoming program on the disk will replace those in the original program.

SYSTEM

This command returns the computer from BASIC to the DOS. It is important to realise that any programs in memory will be lost when this command is executed.

13

Using Data Files

13.1 Data files

When a large amount of common data is required by a program it is inconvenient to enter this data each time via the keyboard. A preferable method is to store the data in DATA statements within the program, as described in Chapter 3. However, this is still restrictive as these DATA statements are not readily available to other programs. The most flexible approach is to store your data in separate files from your programs so that the data files may be used by more than one program. You can then also prepare standard programs to analyse and process different data set up in data files.

A data file is created by a BASIC program so that the contents and format are under your control. In practice this means you are likely to write several programs – for example, one to create the data file, one to update the data file, and some to process the data. This chapter shows how such data files may be created and read.

There are two ways of processing files: sequentially and randomly. Random access of files can only be carried out from disks, whereas sequential access can be carried out from disks or magnetic tape. This book deals only with sequential file systems.

13.2 File records

The contents of a data file may be regarded as the equivalent of a series of DATA statements within a program. Although the data consists of one long 'column' of values, it is useful for you to think and design the logic of your program round the concept of records. For example, a stock record might consist of a stock number, item

description, stock level, unit cost, reorder level and order quantity
as shown in Table 13.1.

Table 13.1 Stock records

Stock No	Description	Stock	Unit Cost	Reorder Level	Order Quantity
1234	Pens	15	45	20	60
2340	Pencils	50	12	40	100
2679	Erasers	8	5	10	50
3456	Rulers	20	26	30	100
4567	Writing pads	40	35	50	200
4568	Notebooks	60	40	30	100
6770	Labels	70	15	25	75
6775	Pins	40	15	20	60
6979	Envelopes	40	20	60	200
7050	Cash books	30	22	40	100

The data contained in Table 13.1, recorded sequentially record
by record, would give rise to a 'column' of values as shown below:

> 1234
> PENS
> 15
> 45
> 20
> 60
> 2340
> PENCILS
> 50
> *etc.*

In transferring this data to and from memory it is more convenient to assign separate variable names to each part of a record
and move one record at a time. This keeps the program logic
simpler, although within a particular program a variable (unit cost,
say) may not be manipulated or used.

As the program examples in this chapter use the data shown in
Table 13.1 this is a convenient place to define the variable names to
be used:

> K = stock number
> D$ = description

S   = stock
C   = unit cost
R   = reorder level
Q   = order quantity

13.3   OPEN and CLOSE statements for data files

All data files used by your program need to be declared before they are used. Prior to reading or writing to a data file, the file needs to be 'opened' by means of an OPEN statement. When all the information has been passed between the file and the computer, the file then needs to be 'closed' by means of a CLOSE statement.

A separate OPEN statement is required for each file to be used in a program, and each file must be identified by a different file number. The general form for an OPEN statement is:

line number OPEN "*filename* FOR *mode* AS #*file number*

For example:

10 OPEN "STOCK" FOR OUTPUT AS #2

The file name may be held in a string variable, for example:

40 INPUT "NAME OF DATA FILE";FT$
50 OPEN FT$ FOR INPUT AS #1

There is usually a limit to the number of files you can have OPEN at any one time. This limit might be a default setting, such as 3 in BASICA. BASICA allows the number to be increased up to a maximum of 15 while in DOS before invoking BASICA. The DOS command is:

BASIC /F:m

where m is the required number of files. Another practice is to provide a MAXFILES statement within the program. For example:

20 MAXFILES = 4

The data file is closed as described previously for print files that is,

line number CLOSE *x*

where

  x = the chosen file number

For example:

    100 CLOSE 1
    110 CLOSE 2

13.4   File input–output statements

The statement used to output a file has the general form:

    PRINT #*filenumber, variable list*

For example:

    PRINT #1,K,D$,S,C,R,Q

The comma as a delimiter is suppressed so that in the above example K,D$,S,C,R,Q, is written as one string. You can preserve the variables separately by using separate PRINT statements, that is:

    PRINT #1,K
    PRINT #1,D$
    PRINT #1,S
    PRINT #1,C
    PRINT #1,R
    PRINT #1,Q

or you can retain the commas by enclosing them in quotes:

    PRINT #1,K;",";D$;",";S;",";C;",";R;",";Q

The corresponding read statement is:

    INPUT #*filenumber, variable list*

Thus a corresponding read statement might be:

    INPUT #1,K,D$,S,C,R,Q

Some systems also provide a WRITE statement that allows the delimiters to be automatically written to the file. For example:

    WRITE #1,K,D$,S,C,R,Q

would automatically introduce a comma on the file between each variable. The programs in this book use the PRINT# form as this is more universally implemented.

13.5   End of file records

It is convenient if you have within your program your own means of detecting the end of the data. This can easily be done by terminating your data files with a dummy record. The contents of this dummy record are chosen to make it unique. For example, in the stock record file previously discussed the dummy stock number could be made larger than any likely to be encountered (i.e. 9999 if four-digit codes are used).

Since a complete record is transferred as a whole, the remaining fields of the dummy record need to be provided with values as shown below:

    9999,X,0,0,0

This can be done in one PRINT statement as:

    PRINT#1,"9999,X,0,0,0"

The general flow of processing when a dummy record is used is shown in Figure 13.1.

13.6   Problems

You should look at the end of the chapter before tackling the problems.

Problem 1–Stock data file

Write a program to create a stock data file incorporating a dummy end record for the data in Table 13.2.

A suitable program is listed in Table A17 (page 156).

Problem 2–Reorder list

Write a program to read the data file produced in Problem 1 and output a list of items to be reordered optionally to the screen or to a printer. A sample output is shown in Table 13.2.

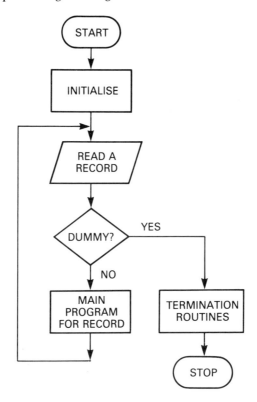

Fig. 13.1   General flow with dummy record

Table 13.2   Output from reorder program

```
                REORDER LIST
                ------------

  CODE        DESCRIPTION       ORDER QTY
  ----        -----------       ---------

  1234        PENS                 60
  2679        ERASERS              50
  3456        RULERS              100
  4567        WRITING PADS        200
  6979        ENVELOPES           200
  7050        CASH BOOKS          100
```

A suitable program is listed in Table A18 (page 157).

Problem 3–A data file search program
Write a program using string functions to search the stock data file produced in Problem 1 for any stock description containing a specified substring (e.g. PEN). An example of the output is shown in Table 13.3.

Table 13.3   Output from search program

```
STOCK FILE SEARCH
---------------------------------------

ENTER SEARCH WORD? PEN
---------------------------------------

CODE     DETAILS      STOCK
---------------------------------------

 1234    PENS            15
 2340    PENCILS         50
---------------------------------------

10 RECORDS READ
 2 RECORDS LISTED
```

Allow for the stock details to be output either to the screen or to the printer. The program is listed in Table A19 (page 158).

14

File Processing and Reporting Example

14.1 Introduction

This chapter describes a stock recording program which is a development of the problem and programs described in Chapter 13. This program also uses the same data. Note however that the data is entered in a different order from that shown in Table 13.1.

The program illustrates the application of many of the programming techniques discussed in this book, and the basic structure of the program is relevant to other applications. The program is menu driven, with all the options being written as subroutines. This will allow further options to be added easily at a later date.

It should be emphasised that this program is given to illustrate programming techniques; it is not intended to be a commercially usable system. A sequential file is used in the example for simplicity.

14.2 The menu

An illustration of the menu is given in Figure 14.1.

The appropriate command (option) is selected by keying in A, C, D, E, R, S, U or V; that is, the initial letter of the required command. A brief description of each command is given below:

ADD   This allows the user to add (that is, create) a further stock record.

CHANGE   This displays an existing stock record and allows any part of its contents to be changed.

DELETE   This allows a stock record to be deleted. It is not

Fig. 14.1   Command menu for stock recording program

deleted from the computer's memory, but instead, the stock description is replaced by the word 'DELETED'. This ensures that it is not saved to the updated file.

EXIT   This terminates the program. Before terminating, the user is given the option of saving the current set of records to tape. Any deleted records will not be saved to the new file.

REORDER REPORT   This produces a stock list of items currently below their reorder level. This list can be displayed on the screen or sent to the printer.

SEARCH   This allows the user to search the stock file for a sub-string match in the stock description field. The output can be directed to the screen or to the printer.

UPDATE STOCK LEVEL   This allows the stock quantity for a specified stock record to be updated.

VALUATION REPORT   This produces a complete stock list, to the screen or printer, giving the value of each stock quantity and a cumulative total for the whole stock holding.

14.3   Structure of the program

All the above menu options have been written as subroutines. In addition, a few routines that are common to these subroutines have been written as 'utility' subroutines. For example, at the end of each option the user is given the choice of repeating the current option or returning to the menu, that is:

Continue or Menu?

Details of all the stock records are held in *arrays*. If a stock file already exists, it is read into the arrays during the 'start up' phase. Stock record changes are made to the array variables, the revised arrays being saved to a file when the EXIT option is chosen.

An outline flowchart is given in Figure 14.2.

A stock record consists of seven fields. They are all numeric fields, except the stock description, and none of them are of fixed length. The fields are as follows:

Stock number: A part or commodity number

Description: Any alphanumeric description

Unit cost: The cost of one unit of stock quantity. The monetary units should be consistent throughout the file.

Order quantity: The standard reorder quantity

Reorder level: Items below this level will appear in the reorder list

Stock quantity: The current stock level. This field can be updated by +/− transactions (i.e. entering a number preceded by a + or − sign).

Stock value: The content of this field is calculated by the program and automatically updated whenever the unit cost or stock quantity is changed.

The listings that might be sent to the printer are: REORDER REPORT, SEARCH and VALUATION REPORT. PRINT USING is used to format the numeric fields so that they are aligned in columns, the financial amounts being presented to two decimal places with the decimal points aligned. The description field plus up to three other fields are formatted to produce a line of not more than 36 characters. If a complete line of characters were used, the cursor would move to the next line on the screen, thereby producing a blank line between each line output.

The program automatically assigns a record number to each stock record, which is, in fact, the array subscript for that record. This record number is not used in any way by the user. The user always

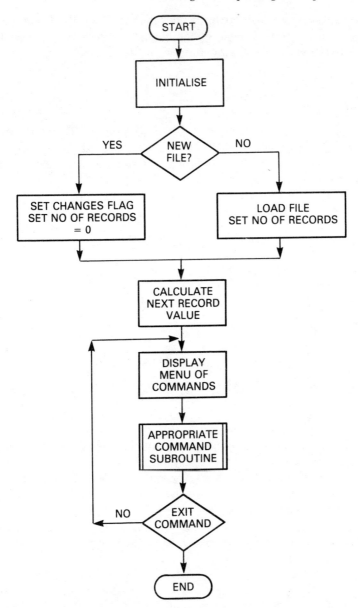

Fig. 14.2 Outline flowchart

references a stock record by its stock number. If the stock number is not known, or has been forgotten, then the SEARCH option on the description field will allow the user to find the appropriate stock number.

14.4   Printed output

Printed output is available for three options: SEARCH, RE-ORDER REPORT and VALUATION REPORT.

The SEARCH option produces a list of all stock items whose description contains the string of characters specified by the user. For each stock item listed, the stock number, description and stock quantity is given. At the end of the listing there is a note of the total number of records searched and a count of those listed. An example of a printed SEARCH listing is given in Table 14.1.

Table 14.1   Example of output for search option

```
        SEARCH FOR BOOKS
----------------------------------------

    STK NO   DESCRIPTION    STK QTY
----------------------------------------

        4568   NOTEBOOKS        60
        7050   CASH BOOKS       30
----------------------------------------
10 RECORDS SEARCHED
2 RECORDS LISTED
```

This option is most likely to be used to find the stock number of an item from its description. The stock quantity is also listed because this is the next most likely reason for accessing a stock record. The number of records searched is given to 'reassure' the user that the whole file has been examined, particularly in the case where no string match has been found.

The REORDER REPORT comprises all those stock items whose current stock quantity is below the reorder level. For each item listed the specified order quantity is given. The program also calculates, from the unit cost and the order quantity, the order cost for each item and cumulates these costs to give a total cost for the complete reorder list. An example of a REORDER REPORT is shown in Table 14.2.

Table 14.2 Example of output for reorder report

```
                REORDER REPORT
                ----------------

STK NO   DESCRIPTION    ORD QTY    COST
----------------------------------------------
   1234  PENS               60  2700.00
   2679  ERASERS            50   250.00
   3456  RULERS            100  2600.00
   4567  WRITING PADS      200  7000.00
   6979  ENVELOPES         200  4000.00
   7050  CASH BOOKS        100  2200.00
----------------------------------------------
                        TOTAL  18750.00
----------------------------------------------
```

The VALUATION REPORT lists all the items in the stock record and presents the current stock quantity together with the value of the stock. A cumulative total of the complete stock value is given at the end of the list as shown in Table 14.3.

Table 14.3 Example of output for valuation report

```
               VALUATION REPORT
               ----------------

STK NO   DESCRIPTION    STK QTY   VALUE
----------------------------------------------
   1234  PENS               15   675.00
   2340  PENCILS            50   600.00
   2679  ERASERS             8    40.00
   3456  RULERS             20   520.00
   4567  WRITING PADS       40  1400.00
   4568  NOTEBOOKS          60  2400.00
   6770  LABELS             70  1050.00
   6775  PINS               40   600.00
   6979  ENVELOPES          40   800.00
   7050  CASH BOOKS         30   660.00
----------------------------------------------
                        TOTAL   8745.00
----------------------------------------------
```

14.5 Initialisation and start-up routine

The initialisation and start-up routine forms the start of the program and this part of the program is shown in Table 14.4. Lines 30 to 90 set up the headings for each field in the stock record. The headings are assigned to elements 1 to 7 in the array H$. To assist in neat screen presentations, all the fields are a fixed 18 characters in length.

Table 14.4 Initialisation and start-up routine

```
10 DIM SN(100),D$(100),UC(100),OQ(100)
20 DIM ROL(100),SL(100),V(100)
30 H$(1)="STOCK NUMBER       "
40 H$(2)="DESCRIPTION         "
50 H$(3)="UNIT COST          "
60 H$(4)="ORDER QUANTITY      "
70 H$(5)="REORDER LEVEL       "
80 H$(6)="STOCK LEVEL         "
90 H$(7)="STOCK VALUE         "
100 SCREEN 0,0
110 CLS
120 PRINT:PRINT
130 PRINT "    New file":PRINT
140 PRINT "OR  Load existing file":PRINT:PRINT
150 INPUT A$
160 IF A$<>"N" AND A$<>"L" THEN 110
170 IF A$="N" THEN N=0
180 IF A$="L" THEN GOSUB 5500:REM LOAD FILE
190 NR=N+1:DC=0
```

Lines 100 to 190 form a start up routine that initialises file record pointers. The user is asked whether the file to be processed is new or is to be loaded as an existing file (lines 130–150). If the file is new, then the number of records (N) is set to zero in line 170. If an existing file is to be loaded, line 180 branches to the file loading subroutine (GOSUB 5500). On returning from the subroutine, the number of records will have been assigned to N. Line 190 completes the initialisation by setting NR (next record variable) to N + 1 and setting DC to zero. DC is a variable that represents the number of records deleted during the course of the run (i.e. delete count).

14.6 File load routine

Table 14.5 File load routine

```
5500 REM FILE LOAD ROUTINE
5510 CLS:PRINT
5520 INPUT "ENTER FILE NAME";FT$
5530 OPEN FT$ FOR INPUT AS #1
5540 PRINT
5550 INPUT #1,N
5560 PRINT
5570 PRINT "READINGS";N;"RECORDS"
5580 FOR I=1 TO N
5590    INPUT #1,SN(I),D$(I),UC(I),OQ(I),ROL(I),SL(I)
5600    V(I)=UC(I)*SL(I)
5610 NEXT I
5620 CLOSE 1:BEEP
5630 RETURN
```

The file load routine is given in Table 14.5. On entering the file load routine the user is asked to input the file name. Line 5530 opens the file for reading from disk. Once opened, the first data item is read from the file as a value for N, the total number of records. A loop is then set up between lines 5580 and 5610 to read N sets of records into six arrays. The file is then closed (line 5620) and a beep sounded to confirm the file has closed.

The six variable names are:

SN(I)	Stock number
D$(I)	Description
UC(I)	Unit cost
OQ(I)	Order quantity
ROL(I)	Reorder level
SL(I)	Stock quantity (i.e. level)

A seventh variable V(I), stock value, is calculated within the loop, thereby ensuring that the stock value held in memory is based upon the latest situation. After reading in all the records, the subroutine returns to the start-up routine at line 190 as previously described.

14.7   Main program and menu

The main program and menu subroutine are shown in Table 14.6.

The main program only occupies five lines, 400 to 440. The first line (400) calls the menu subroutine which return a value for OP depending upon the option selected. The main program in line 420 then branches to the appropriate option subroutine. Having completed the option the program returns to line 430. The exit option would have set OP to equal 4, therefore if OP does not equal 4 the program loops back to line 400 and presents the menu once again. If the exit option has been selected and therefore OP does equal 4, then the program goes instead to line 440 which halts execution.

The subroutine starting at line 1200 displays the menu and sets the value of OP according to the option selected. Lines 1220 and 1290 are PRINT statements that set up the screen display of menu options. These options are referred to as 'commands' on the menu and the user makes his selection by entering the initial letter (i.e. A,C,D,E,R,S,U or V). Line 1330 compares the input from the user

Table 14.6 Main program and menu subroutine

```
400 GOSUB 1200:REM MENU
410 CLS
420 ON OP GOSUB 1500,2500,2000,6000,4000,3000,3500,4500
430 IF OP<>4 THEN 400
440 END




1200 REM MENU
1210 CLS
1220 PRINT "            COMMAND MENU"
1230 PRINT
1240 PRINT "     Add              Change":PRINT
1250 PRINT "     Delete           Search":PRINT
1260 PRINT "       Update stock level":PRINT
1270 PRINT "        Reorder report":PRINT
1280 PRINT "        Valuation report":PRINT
1290 PRINT "        Exit program":PRINT
1300 INPUT "     COMMAND ACDERSUV";A$
1310 OP=0
1320 FOR I=1 TO 8
1330    IF A$=MID$("ACDERSUV",I,1) THEN OP=I
1340 NEXT I
1350 IF OP<1 OR OP>8 THEN 1200
1360 RETURN
```

with successive letters in the string 'ACDERSUV' and sets the variable OP accordingly (e.g. OP = 1, OP = 2 for C, etc.). Finally, line 1350 checks that the value allocated to OP lies between 1 and 8; if not, the program returns to the start of the subroutine at line 1200.

The subroutines associated with the menu options will be described in alphabetical order.

Add record routine

The add record subroutine is shown in Table 14.7, together with two associated subroutines. The add record subroutine starts by displaying the record number. Although this is not directly used by the user, it is useful to know the size of the file when adding further records. Lines 1530 to 1580 display the stock record headings in turn and require the user to make an appropriate entry. When all the data for a new stock record has been input, line 1590 asks the user whether the data should be accepted. The data has been stored in temporary variables. If the data is accepted, then the record number

Table 14.7 Add record routine

```
1500 REM ADD RECORD
1510 CLS
1520 PRINT "RECORD NO";NR:PRINT:PRINT
1530 PRINT H$(1);:INPUT SN:PRINT
1540 PRINT H$(2);:INPUT D$:PRINT:D$=LEFT$(D$,12)
1550 PRINT H$(3);:INPUT UC:PRINT
1560 PRINT H$(4);:INPUT OQ:PRINT
1570 PRINT H$(5);:INPUT ROL:PRINT
1580 PRINT H$(6);:INPUT SL:PRINT
1590 INPUT "ACCEPT DATA Y/N";A$
1600 IF A$<>"Y" THEN 1640
1610 XX=NR
1620 GOSUB 8000:REM SET UP RECORD
1630 NR=NR+1
1640 GOSUB 7200
1650 IF A$="C" THEN 1500
1660 RETURN



8000 REM SET UP RECORD
8010 SN(XX)=SN
8020 D$(XX)=D$
8030 UC(XX)=UC
8040 OQ(XX)=OQ
8050 ROL(XX)=ROL
8060 SL(XX)=SL
8070 V(XX)=SL(XX)*UC(XX)
8080 RETURN



7200 REM CONTINUE
7210 PRINT
7220 INPUT "Continue or Menu";A$
7230 RETURN
```

(NR) is transferred to a temporary variable XX prior to the program going to subroutine 8000 that sets the record up in the required array elements. Having set up the record, the record counter is increased by 1 in line 1630. Another subroutine is then called that determines whether the user wishes to continue using this option (i.e. adding records) or to return to the menu. The subroutine is called in line

1640 and returns the variable A$ as a character C or M. If A$ = "C" then the subroutine is repeated from line 1500, otherwise control passes back to the main program (to line 430).

When the additional record data is not accepted in line 1590, then line 1600 causes the program to go to line 1640 without entering the temporary data into array elements. The user can then either repeat the option and enter acceptable data or return to the main menu.

It should be noted that the stock value is calculated within the 'set up record' subroutine in line 8070. The stock value is therefore only calculated and stored once the data has been accepted.

Change record routine

The change record subroutine is given in Table 14.8, together with the cursor move subroutine. To change the details within an existing stock record the user has to specify the stock number (line 2520). A FOR . . . NEXT loop is then executed over lines 2530 to 2800 to search sequentially through the stock number array SN. If no match is found in line 2540 a jump is made to NEXT I to increase the array subscript, I, by one. When a match is found, the statements within the loop are executed. None of these statements cause a jump out of the loop, so that even when a match has been found and acted on, the search for similar records with the same stock number continues to the end of the file. Although there should not be two stock records with the same stock number, if such a situation arose, this subroutine would highlight the fact and the situation could be remedied by using either the change record option or the delete record option.

Within the loop, each field heading is displayed in turn together with the current contents for that record (e.g. line 2560). The length of the field is evaluated (e.g. line 2570) and subroutine 7600 is then used to reposition the cursor over the initial character. To re-enter an existing entry, move the cursor to the right of the entry and press the return key to store it in a temporary variable; alternatively any changes made prior to pressing the return key will be input to the temporary variable (e.g. line 2580). Each field is treated in a similar manner until finally line 2750 is reached. If the 'data', as displayed and edited, is now accepted (i.e. A$ = "Y") then the stock value is re-calculated in line 2780 and line 2790 calls subroutine 8000 to

Table 14.8 Change record routine

```
2500 REM CHANGE RECORD
2510 CLS
2520 INPUT "STOCK NO TO CHANGE";SN
2530 FOR I=1 TO NR-1
2540    IF SN(I)<>SN THEN 2800
2550    PRINT:PRINT "RECORD NO";I:PRINT
2560    PRINT H$(1);SN(I);
2570    L=LEN(STR$(SN(I)))+2
2580    GOSUB 7600:INPUT SN
2590    PRINT H$(2);" "+D$(I);
2600    L=LEN(D$(I))+2
2610    GOSUB 7600:INPUT D$:D$=LEFT$(D$,12)
2620    PRINT H$(3);UC(I);
2630    L=LEN(STR$(UC(I)))+2
2640    GOSUB 7600:INPUT UC
2650    PRINT H$(4);OQ(I);
2660    L=LEN(STR$(OQ(I)))+2
2670    GOSUB 7600:INPUT OQ
2680    PRINT H$(5);ROL(I);
2690    L=LEN(STR$(ROL(I)))+2
2700    GOSUB 7600:INPUT ROL
2710    PRINT H$(6);SL(I);
2720    L=LEN(STR$(SL(I)))+2
2730    GOSUB 7600:INPUT SL
2740    PRINT
2750    INPUT "ACCEPT DATA Y/N";A$
2760    IF A$<>"Y" THEN 2800
2770    IF D$(I)<>"**DELETED**" THEN 2780
2775    IF D$<>"**DELETED**" THEN DR=DR-1
2780    V(I)=SL(I)*UC(I)
2790    XX=I:GOSUB 8000
2800 NEXT I
2810 GOSUB 7200
2820 IF A$="C" THEN 2500
2830 RETURN




7600 REM CURSOR MOVE
7610 ZX=POS(1)-L
7620 ZY=CSRLIN
7630 LOCATE ZY,ZX
7640 RETURN
```

transfer the values from the temporary variables to the appropriate array elements. If the data is not accepted, this transfer does not take place and a jump is made to the end of the loop (to line 2800).

Having processed one change, the final lines of the change record subroutine allow the user to continue making changes, or to return to the main menu.

Note that the cursor move subroutine (lines 7600–7640) uses two new functions: POS(1), which returns the current cursor position; and CSRLIN, which returns the vertical coordinate of the cursor. Line 7610 therefore calculates how many column positions the cursor has to move to the left (L being, for example, the length of the current description +2 calculated in the change record subroutine at line 2600) and stores this in the variable ZX as the x coordinate of the cursor. Line 7620 stores the current y coordinate of the cursor position (i.e. row number) in ZY. ZX and ZY are used in the LOCATE statement (line 7630) to position the cursor at the required place on the screen ready for the next INPUT (e.g. at line 2610).

Delete record routine

The delete record and display record subroutines are shown in Table 14.9. The record to be deleted is identified by entering its stock number (line 2020). Each record within the file is then examined in turn for a match with the stock number within the loop 2030 to 2140. When a match is found, a 'DELETE THIS RECORD' message is displayed. The relevant record details are displayed by calling the subroutine at 7400 from line 2080.

The subroutine at 7400 displays the record number, field headings and their contents. Having displayed the record the user is asked if he is sure that he wishes the record to be deleted (line 2090). If the response is N (No) then no action is taken and the program jumps to the end of the loop (i.e. NEXT I at 2140). On the other hand, if the response is Y (Yes), then line 2120 replaces the current stock description with the string '**DELETED**' and line 2130 increases the deleted records count by one.

The record is therefore not deleted immediately, but a flag is put into the stock description field which will allow the record to be identified during the file saving routine. The record will not be saved

Table 14.9 Delete record routine

```
2000 REM DELETE RECORD
2010 CLS
2020 INPUT "STOCK NO TO DELETE";SND
2030 FOR I=1 TO NR-1
2040     IF SN(I)<>SND THEN 2140
2050     X=I
2060     CLS
2070     PRINT "          DELETE THIS RECORD"
2080     GOSUB 7400:REM DISPLAY RECORD
2090     PRINT:INPUT "ARE YOU SURE Y/N";A$
2100     IF A$="N" THEN 2140
2110     IF A$<>"Y" THEN 2060
2120     D$(I)="**DELETED**"
2130     DR=DR+1
2140 NEXT I
2150 GOSUB 7200
2160 IF A$="C" THEN 2000
2170 RETURN



7400 REM DISPLAY RECORD
7410 PRINT "RECORD NO";X:PRINT
7420 PRINT H$(1);SN(X):PRINT
7430 PRINT H$(2);" "+D$(X):PRINT
7440 PRINT H$(3);UC(X):PRINT
7450 PRINT H$(4);OQ(X):PRINT
7460 PRINT H$(5);ROL(X):PRINT
7470 PRINT H$(6);SL(X):PRINT
7480 PRINT H$(7);V(X):PRINT
7490 RETURN
```

on the updated file. This approach allows the user to use the SEARCH option just prior to exiting the program and search for the string '**DELETED**'. A complete list of records about to be dropped from the updated file can then be obtained. If the user has any second thoughts about stock items appearing on the list he can then use the CHANGE RECORD option to replace the '**DELETED**' in the stock description by its proper description once again and the record will not then be dropped.

As with the other options, the lines 2150 to 2170 allow the user to continue with the DELETE option or to return to the menu.

Exit program routine

Table 14.10 Exit program routine

```
6000 REM EXIT & SAVE ROUTINE
6010 CLS
6020 INPUT "SAVE CURRENT FILE Y/N";A$
6030 IF A$<>"N" AND A$<>"Y" THEN 6000
6040 IF A$="N" THEN 6160
6050 PRINT
6060 INPUT "ENTER FILE NAME";FT$
6070 OPEN FT$ FOR OUTPUT AS #1
6080 PRINT #1,NR-1-DR
6090 FOR I=1 TO NR-1
6100     IF D$(I)="**DELETED**" THEN 6130
6110        PRINT #1,SN(I);",";D$(I);",";UC(I)
6120        PRINT #1,OQ(I);",";ROL(I);",";SL(I)
6130 NEXT I
6140 CLOSE 1
6150 PRINT "FILE SAVED":BEEP
6160 RETURN
```

The exit program subroutine is shown in Table 14.10. When this option is chosen from the main menu the user is asked in line 6020 whether he wishes to save the current file. If the response is N (No) then the program jumps to the end of this subroutine (i.e. line 6160). If the response is Y (Yes) the main part of the subroutine is executed. If the response is neither N nor Y, then line 6030 ensures that the question is repeated until a N or Y response is obtained.

The main part of the subroutine lies between lines 6060 and 6150. Line 6060 requests the name of the proposed file. Line 6070 opens the file for writing.

The first data item to be recorded, in line 6080, is the total number of records to be saved, the total number being the current number of records, NR − 1, less the number of deleted records. Lines 6090 to 6130 form a loop that processes each record in turn. If the record is a 'deleted' record then line 6100 causes that record to be bypassed, otherwise each field of the record is written to the file over lines 6110 to 6120. Only the calculated 'value of stock' is not written to the file. After processing all the records, line 6140 closes the file and line 6150 displays a message confirming that the file has been saved; a beep is then sounded.

Reorder report routine

The reorder report routine is shown in Table 14.11 together with an associated subroutine (starting at line 7800). The reorder report subroutine starts by having line 4020 call the subroutine at 7800. This allows the user to set the output device to be either the screen or the printer. Line 4030 then opens the appropriate device. The

Table 14.11   Reorder report routine

```
4000 REM REORDER REPORT
4010 CLS
4020 GOSUB 7800
4030 OPEN A$ FOR OUTPUT AS #1
4040 CT=0
4050 PRINT #1,"   "
4060 PRINT #1,"            REORDER REPORT"
4070 PRINT #1,"            ---------------"
4080 PRINT #1,"   "
4090 PRINT #1,"STK NO  DESCRIPTION    ORD QTY   COST"
4100 PRINT #1,"---------------------------------------"
4110 FOR I=1 TO NR-1
4120    IF SL(I)>ROL(I) THEN 4190
4130    CST=OQ(I)*UC(I)
4140    CT=CT+CST
4150    PRINT #1,USING"######";SN(I);
4160    PRINT #1,SPC(2);D$(I);SPC(12-LEN(D$(I)));
4170    PRINT #1,USING"########";OQ(I);
4180    PRINT #1,USING"#####.##";CST
4190 NEXT I
4200 PRINT #1,"---------------------------------------"
4210 PRINT #1,"            TOTAL ";
4220 PRINT #1,USING"######.##";CT
4230 PRINT #1,"---------------------------------------"
4240 CLOSE 1
4250 GOSUB 7200
4260 IF A$="C" THEN 4000
4270 RETURN


7800 REM SET UP OUTPUT DEVICE
7810 PRINT
7820 INPUT "OUTPUT TO SCREEN OR PRINTER, S/P";B$
7830 IF B$="S" THEN A$="SCRN:"
7840 IF B$="P" THEN A$="LPT1:"
7850 IF B$<>"S" AND B$<>"P" THEN 7820
7860 RETURN
```

cumulative monetary total (CT) is set to zero in line 4040 and then the report headings are printed (lines 4060–4100).

The individual records are processed, in turn, within the loop set up by lines 4110 and 4190. If the stock level is above the reorder level a jump is made to the end of the loop, from line 4120 to 4190. If a stock item is to be listed, then the cost of the stock order (CST) is calculated, in line 4130, by multiplying the order quantity by the unit cost. The cumulative cost is updated in line 4140 and the results for one stock record are printed in lines 4150 to 4180.

Having processed all the records in the file, the loop, lines 4110 to 4190, is left and the final stages of the report produced. Line 4200 underlines the stock list. The cumulative cost is printed out in line 4220. Finally line 4230 underlines the cumulative cost, and the output file is closed in line 4240. The user can then repeat the report by 'continuing' or return to the main menu.

In practice, the user might send the report to the screen first, to check its contents and then, if satisfied, 'continue' and send the report to the printer.

Search records routine

The search records subroutine is shown in Table 14.12. The user is requested to enter the required search string at line 3040. The length of the search string is calculated in line 3050 and two search parameters, E and F, set to zero. Line 3070 allows the user to specify the output device and line 3080 opens the output file. The report headings are printed out over lines 3100 to 3140. Each record is processed within the loop at lines 3150 to 3270.

As each record is examined, the record count, E, is increased by one in line 3160. Line 3170 calculates W, the number of successive comparisons of the search string that can be made within the stock description string. The string comparisons for one record are then made within the loop over lines 3180 to 3260. A sub-string of the stock description extracted at line 3190 is compared with the search string at line 3200. If a match is found, then the 'number found' count, F, is increased by one at line 3210. Details of the record are printed in lines 3220 to 3240, and the loop is 'closed' by setting P to the end value W in line 3250.

Having processed each record the output is concluded by reporting the number of records searched and the number of matches

Table 14.12 Search records routine

```
3000 REM SEARCH ROUTINE
3010 CLS
3020 PRINT "STOCK FILE SEARCH"
3025 PRINT "------------------"
3030 PRINT
3040 INPUT "ENTER SEARCH STRING";X$
3050 L=LEN(X$):E=0:F=0:XX=0
3060 PRINT
3070 GOSUB 7800
3080 OPEN A$ FOR OUTPUT AS #1
3090 PRINT #1,"   "
3100 PRINT #1,"      SEARCH FOR ";X$
3110 PRINT #1,"-----------------------------------"
3120 PRINT #1,"  "
3130 PRINT #1," STK NO  DESCRIPTION   STK QTY"
3140 PRINT #1,"-----------------------------------"
3150 FOR I=1 TO NR-1
3160    E=E+1
3170    W=LEN(D$(I))-L+1
3180    FOR P=1 TO W
3190       Z$=MID$(D$(I),P,L)
3200       IF Z$<>X$ THEN 3260
3210       F=F+1
3220       PRINT #1,USING "########";SN(I);
3230       PRINT #1,SPC(2);D$(I);SPC(11-LEN(D$(I)));
3240       PRINT #1,USING "########";SL(I)
3250       P=W
3260    NEXT P
3270 NEXT I
3280 PRINT #1,"-----------------------------------"
3290 PRINT #1,E;"RECORDS SEARCHED"
3300 PRINT #1,F;"RECORDS LISTED"
3310 CLOSE 1
3320 GOSUB 7200
3330 IF A$="C" THEN 3000
3340 RETURN
```

found (lines 3280–3300). The output file is then closed at line 3310 and the user continues with another search or returns to the main menu.

Update stock routine

The update stock subroutine is shown in Table 14.13. Having specified the stock number in line 3520, the stock records are searched within the loop, line 3540 to line 3680. Line 3550 ensures that records not specified are by-passed. When an appropriate record is found, its record number, stock number and description

Table 14.13   Update stock routine

```
3500 REM STOCK UPDATE
3510 CLS
3520 INPUT "STOCK NO TO UPDATE";SN
3530 PRINT
3540 FOR I=1 TO NR-1
3550    IF SN(I)<>SN THEN 3680
3560    PRINT "RECORD NO";I:PRINT
3570    PRINT H$(1);SN(I):PRINT
3580    PRINT H$(2);" ";D$(I):PRINT
3590    PRINT "CURRENT STOCK     ";SL(I):PRINT
3600    SA=0
3610    INPUT "STOCK ADJUSTMENT +/-";SA:PRINT
3620    SL=SL(I)+SA
3630    PRINT "REVISED STOCK     ";SL:PRINT
3640    INPUT "ACCEPT DATA Y/N";A$
3650    IF A$<>"Y" THEN 3680
3660    SL(I)=SL
3670    V(I)=SL(I)*UC(I)
3680 NEXT I
3690 GOSUB 7200
3700 IF A$="C" THEN 3500
3710 RETURN
```

are printed by lines 3560 to 3580. The current stock level is printed by line 3590, the stock adjustment (SA) set to zero in line 3600, and an adjustment requested from the user in line 3610. A temporary variable (SL) is then used to hold the revised stock level and its value is printed by line 3630. If the adjustment is not accepted by the user in line 3640, then line 3650 by-passes the updating and the processing continues within the loop to the next record.

Accepted revised records are updated by transferring the stock level in the temporary variable to the correct array element (line 3660) and by the re-calculation of the value of stock (line 3670). The routine ends with the standard 'continue' or return to main menu option.

Valuation report routine
The valuation report subroutine is shown in Table 14.14. The valuation report routine is similar to the reorder report routine. Lines 4520 and 4530 allow the user to send the report to the screen or the printer. The cumulative total is set to zero in line 4540 and then the report headings are printed out over lines 4560 to 4600.

Table 14.14 Valuation report routine

```
4500 REM VALUATION REPORT
4510 CLS
4520 GOSUB 7800
4530 OPEN A$ FOR OUTPUT AS #1
4540 CT=0
4550 PRINT #1," "
4560 PRINT #1,"              VALUATION REPORT"
4570 PRINT #1,"              ------------------"
4580 PRINT #1," "
4590 PRINT #1,"STK NO  DESCRIPTION    STK QTY   VALUE"
4600 PRINT #1,"-----------------------------------------"
4610 FOR I=1 TO NR-1
4620    PRINT #1,USING"######";SN(I);
4630    PRINT #1,SPC(2);D$(I);SPC(12-LEN(D$(I)));
4640    PRINT #1,USING"#########";SL(I);
4650    PRINT #1,USING"#####.##";V(I)
4660    CT=CT+V(I)
4670 NEXT I
4680 PRINT #1,"-----------------------------------------"
4690 PRINT #1,"                        TOTAL ";
4700 PRINT #1,USING"######.##";CT
4710 PRINT #1,"-----------------------------------------"
4720 CLOSE 1
4730 GOSUB 7200
4740 IF A$="C" THEN 4500
4750 RETURN
```

Each record is printed out in the loop (lines 4620–4650). The cumulative stock value is updated in line 4660.

Having printed out all the stock records, the cumulative stock value and the bottom lines of the report are printed out over lines 4680 to 4710. The routine ends in the standard way by giving the user the option to continue, perhaps to obtain a second copy of the report, or to return to the main menu.

Appendix A

Programs (Tables A1–A19)

Table A1   Number of £s required

```
5 CLS
10 INPUT "A,E,P,N,R";A,E,P,N,R
20 PRINT
30 LET T=((A+E)*N+P)/R
40 PRINT "LENGTH OF STAY(NIGHTS)        : ";N
50 PRINT "ACCOMODATION(PER NIGHT)    $: ";A
60 PRINT "EXPENSES(MEALS ETC.)       $: ";E
70 PRINT "ALLOWANCE FOR PRESENTS     $: ";P
80 PRINT "EXCHANGE RATE($ TO THE  £ ) : ";R
90 PRINT
100 PRINT "POUNDS STERLING REQUIRED   : ";
110 PRINT USING"###.##";T
120 PRINT "*********************************"
```

Table A2   Cost of stationery

```
5 CLS
10 INPUT "NO OF DELEGATES";N
20 INPUT "COST OF FOLDERS AND PADS";F,P
30 INPUT "COST OF PENS AND DISCOUNT";S,D
40 PRINT:PRINT
50 LET C=N*(F+P+2*S*(100-D)/100)/100
60 PRINT "NO OF DELEGATES         : ";N
70 PRINT "COST OF FOLDERS         : ";F;"P EACH"
80 PRINT "COST OF PAPER           : ";P;"P PER PAD"
90 PRINT "COST OF PENS LESS";D"% : ";S;"P EACH"
100 PRINT
110 PRINT "TOTAL COST OF STATIONERY = £ ";
120 PRINT USING"##.##";C
130 PRINT "*********************************"
```

Table A3 Using the ON . . . GOTO statement

```
5 CLS
10 PRINT "CALCULATIONS FOR DIFFERENT CODES"
20 PRINT "----------------------------------"
30 PRINT
40 INPUT "NUMBER OF SETS OF DATA";N
50 PRINT:PRINT
60 FOR I=1 TO N
70    INPUT "CODE,X,Y";C,X,Y
80    PRINT:PRINT
90    ON C GOTO 100,110,120,130,140
100   R=X+Y:GOTO 150
110   R=X-Y:GOTO 150
120   R=X*Y:GOTO 150
130   R=X/Y:GOTO 150
140   R=X^Y
150   PRINT "CODE: ";C;"   RESULT =";R
160   PRINT "************************"
170   PRINT:PRINT
180 NEXT I
```

Table A4 Centring a rectangle

```
10 CLS
20 INPUT "WIDTH,DEPTH OF SCREEN";WI,DE
30 INPUT "WIDTH,DEPTH OF RECTANGLE";W,D
40 S=INT(WI/2)-INT(W/2)
50 CLS
60 FOR I=1 TO INT(DE/2)-INT(D/2)
70    PRINT
80 NEXT I
85 PRINT TAB(S);
90 FOR I=1 TO W
100   PRINT "-";
110 NEXT I
120 FOR I=1 TO D-2
130    PRINT TAB(S);"I";TAB(W-1+S);"I"
140 NEXT I
145 PRINT TAB(S);
150 FOR I=1 TO W
160    PRINT "-";
170 NEXT I
```

Table A5   Radius of circumcircle

```
10 INPUT "SIDES OF TRIANGLE";A,B,C
20 PRINT
30 X=(A*A+C*C-B*B)/(2*A*C)
40 R=B/(2*SIN(ATN(SQR(1-X*X)/X)))
50 PRINT
60 PRINT "RADIUS =";
70 PRINT USING"####.###";R;
80 PRINT " M"
90 PRINT "*****************"
```

Table A6   Volumes of solids

```
5 CLS
10 DATA CUBOID,CYLINDER,"HEX BAR"
20 DEF FNR(A)=INT(A/F+.5)*F
30 INPUT "ENTER CODE AND SCALE";C,F
40 IF C=0 THEN END
50 INPUT "ENTER TWO DIMENSIONS";D1,D2
60 INPUT "ENTER HEIGHT";H
70 PRINT
80 ON C GOTO 90,100,110
90 A=D1*D2:GOTO 120
100 A=3.142*D1*D1:GOTO 120
110 A=SQR(27)/2*D1*D1
120 FOR I=1 TO C
130    READ N$
140 NEXT I
150 PRINT "VOL OF ";N$;"=";
160 PRINT FNR(A*H);" CUBIC CM"
170 PRINT "************************"
180 PRINT:PRINT
190 RESTORE
200 GOTO 30
```

Table A7   Copying an array

```
10 INPUT "NO OF ELEMENTS IN ARRAY";N
20 PRINT:PRINT
30 DIM A(20),B(20)
40 FOR I=1 TO N
50    READ A(I)
60 NEXT I
70 FOR I=1 TO N STEP 5
80    FOR J=I TO I+4
90       B(J)=A(N+1-J)
100      PRINT B(J);
110   NEXT J
120   PRINT
130 NEXT I
140 DATA 1,2,3,4,5,6,7,8,9,10,11,12,13
150 DATA 14,15,16,17,18,19,20
```

Table A8   Sum of elements

```
10 DIM A(5,5)
20 INPUT "ENTER M FOR M x M ARRAY";M
30 IF M=0 THEN END
40 D=0
50 FOR I=1 TO M
60    FOR J=1 TO M
70       READ A(I,J)
80       PRINT A(I,J);
90    NEXT J
100   PRINT
110   D=D+A(I,I)+A(I,M+1-I)
120 NEXT I
130 PRINT
140 IF M/2=INT(M/2) THEN 160
150 N=INT(M/2)+1:D=D-A(N,N)
160 PRINT "SUM ON DIAGONALS =";D
170 PRINT "************************"
180 PRINT:PRINT
190 RESTORE
200 GOTO 20
210 DATA 10,11,12,13,14,15,16,17
220 DATA 18,19,20,21,22,23,24,25
230 DATA 26,27,28,29,30,31,32,33,34
```

Table A9   Sorting a list of numbers

```
10 INPUT "NO OF NUMBERS";N
20 CLS
30 DIM A(11)
40 FOR I=1 TO N
50    READ A(I):PRINT A(I);
60 NEXT I
70 PRINT
80 FOR I=1 TO N-1
90    E=0
100   FOR J=1 TO N-1
110      IF A(J)>A(J+1) THEN SWAP A(J),A(J+1):E=1
120   NEXT J
130   IF E=0 THEN END
140   FOR K=1 TO N
150      PRINT A(K);
160   NEXT K
170   PRINT
180 NEXT I
190 DATA 5,3,20,22,22,9,4,23,2,0,-2
```

Table A10   Plot of percentage pastureland

```
5 CLS
10 DIM V(100)
20 INPUT "ENTER NO OF YEARS";N
30 PRINT
40 FOR I=1 TO N
50    PRINT "% PASTURELAND, YR";I;
60    INPUT V(I)
70 NEXT I
80 PRINT
90 GOSUB 1010
100 END
```

Table A11   Pastureland histogram

```
5 CLS
10 DIM V(100),X(15),F(15)
20 INPUT "ENTER NO OF PARISHES";N
30 PRINT
40 FOR I=1 TO N
50    PRINT "PARISH";I;
60    INPUT V(I)
70 NEXT I
80 PRINT
90 GOSUB 2000
100 GOSUB 3000:END
110 GOSUB 4000:END
```

Table A12   Input subroutine

```
800 PRINT
810 INPUT "NO OF ROWS IN FREQ DIST.";N
820 IF N < 11 THEN 850
830 PRINT "NOT MORE THAN 10, TRY AGAIN"
840 GOTO 800
850 PRINT
860 PRINT "INPUT X & CUM FREQ"
870 FOR I=1 TO N
880    INPUT D(I,1),D(I,2)
890 NEXT I
895 RETURN
```

Table A13   Timer alarm

```
10 GOSUB 200
20 CLS
30 LOCATE 8,6
40 PRINT"SET DURATION   ";T$
50 LOCATE 12,6
60 PRINT"ELAPSED TIME"
70 REM TICK AWAY
80 PLAY"O6 B"
90 REM ELAPSED TIME
100 LOCATE 12,20
110 PRINT TIME$
120 IF TIME$<>T$ THEN 70
130 LOCATE 16,6
140 PRINT"PRESS SPACE BAR TO STOP"
150 PLAY"O2 L64 CB"
160 LOCATE 12,20
170 PRINT TIME$
180 IF INKEY$<>" " THEN 150
190 END
200 REM SET UP TIMER DURATION
210 CLS
220 PRINT"SET TIMER DURATION"
230 PRINT
240 INPUT"NUMBER OF MINUTES & SEC AS MM:SS ",M$
250 IF LEN(M$)<>5 THEN 240
260 IF VAL(RIGHT$(M$,2))>60 THEN 240
270 IF VAL(LEFT$(M$,2))>60 THEN 240
280 T$="00:"+M$
290 PRINT
300 PRINT"PRESS SPACE BAR TO START"
310 IF INKEY$="" THEN 310
320 TIME$="0"
330 RETURN
```

Table A14   Cos X

```
10 CLS:PRINT:PRINT
20 INPUT "NO OF TERMS FOR COS X";N
30 INPUT "VALUE OF X (DEGREES)";X1
40 X=(X1*3.142/180)^2
50 T=1:C=1
60 FOR I=2 TO N*2 STEP 2
70    T=(-1)*T*X/((I-1)*I)
80    C=C+T
90 NEXT I
100 PRINT
110 PRINT "COS";X1;"=";
115 PRINT USING"##.######";C
120 PRINT "*****************"
```

Table A15   Roots of quadratic equations

```
10 CLS
20 PRINT "ROOTS OF QUADRATIC EQUATIONS"
30 PRINT "-----------------------------"
40 INPUT "ENTER A,B,C  (ZEROS TO STOP)";A,B,C
50 IF A=0 THEN END
60 D=B*B-4*A*C
70 IF D<0 THEN 150
80 IF D=0 THEN 160
90 D=SQR(D)
100 PRINT "REAL ROOTS:  ";
110 PRINT USING"##.##";((-B+D)/(2*A));
120 PRINT "  AND  ";
130 PRINT USING "##.##";((-B-D)/(2*A))
140 GOTO 180
150 PRINT "COMPLEX ROOTS":GOTO 180
160 PRINT "COINCIDENT ROOTS: ";
170 PRINT USING"##.##";(-B/(2*A))
180 PRINT "******************************"
190 PRINT
200 GOTO 40
```

Table A16 Width of a slit

```
10 CLS
20 PRINT "WIDTH OF A SLIT"
30 PRINT "-----------------"
40 INPUT "ENTER WAVELENGTH";L
50 PRINT
60 INPUT "ENTER NO OF FRINGES";N
70 FOR I=1 TO N
80    PRINT "ENTER TWO PAIRS OF VERNIER READINGS"
90    PRINT "(DEG,MIN FOR EACH) FOR FRINGE NO";I
100   FOR J=1 TO 2
110      INPUT P(I,J),Q(I,J),R(I,J),S(I,J)
120      B(J)=P(I,J)*60+Q(I,J)-R(I,J)*60-S(I,J)
130   NEXT J
140   A(I)=(B(1)+B(2))/4
150   W(I)=I*L*60*180/(A(I)*3.142)
160 NEXT I
170 PRINT
180 PRINT "FRINGE VERNIER READINGS   A   WIDTH OF"
190 PRINT "NUMBER DEG MIN  DEG MIN MIN SLIT   CM"
200 PRINT "-------------------------------------------"
210 FOR I=1 TO N
220   W(I)=INT(W(I)/.0001+.5)*.0001
230   PRINT TAB(7);P(I,1);TAB(12);Q(I,1);
240   PRINT TAB(16);R(I,1);TAB(21);S(I,1)
250   PRINT TAB(2);I;TAB(25);A(I);TAB(30);W(I)
260   PRINT TAB(7);P(I,2);TAB(12);Q(I,2);
270   PRINT TAB(16);R(I,2);TAB(21);S(I,2)
280   PRINT "-------------------------------------------"
290   PRINT
300   W=W+W(I)
310 NEXT I
320 PRINT
330 W=INT(W/N/.0001+.5)*.0001
340 PRINT "WIDTH OF SLIT =";W"CM"
350 PRINT "************************"
```

Table A17   Stock data file creation

```
10 REM CREATES STOCK FILE
20 DIM K(20),D$(20),S(20),C(20),R(20),Q(20)
30 I=0
40 CLS:PRINT
50 PRINT"STOCK FILE CREATION"
60 PRINT"--------------------"
70 PRINT
80 I=I+1
90 PRINT"RECORD NO        ";I
100 INPUT"CODE            ";K(I)
110 IF K(I)=9999 THEN 180
120 INPUT"DESCRIPTION     ";D$(I)
130 INPUT"STOCK LEVEL     ";S(I)
140 INPUT"UNIT COST       ";C(I)
150 INPUT"RE-ORDER LEVEL";R(I)
160 INPUT"ORDER QUANTITY";Q(I)
170 GOTO 40
180 CLS
190 INPUT"ENTER FILE NAME";FT$
200 OPEN FT$ FOR OUTPUT AS #1
210 FOR N=1 TO I-1
220     PRINT #1,K(N);",";D$(N);",";S(N);",";
230     PRINT #1,C(N);",";R(N);",";Q(N)
240 NEXT N
250 PRINT #1,"9999,X,0,0,0,0"
260 CLOSE 1
```

Table A18 Reorder list

```
10 REM PRODUCES A REORDER LIST
20 SCREEN 0:CLS:PRINT
30 DIM K(20),D$(20),S(20),C(20),R(20),Q(20)
40 INPUT"NAME OF DATA FILE";FT$
50 OPEN FT$ FOR INPUT AS #1
60 GOSUB 7800
70 OPEN A$ FOR OUTPUT AS #2
80 FOR I=1 TO 20
90     INPUT #1,K(I),D$(I),S(I),C(I),R(I),Q(I)
100     IF K(I)=9999 THEN 120
110 NEXT I
120 CLOSE 1:BEEP:CLS:PRINT
130 PRINT #2,TAB(12);"REORDER LIST"
140 PRINT #2,TAB(12);"------------"
150 PRINT #2," "
160 PRINT #2,TAB(1);"CODE";SPC(5);"DESCRIPTION";
170 PRINT #2,SPC(5);"ORDER QTY"
180 PRINT #2,TAB(1);"----";SPC(5);"-----------";
190 PRINT #2,SPC(5);"---------"
200 PRINT #2," "
210 FOR I=1 TO 20
220     IF K(I)=9999 THEN 260
230     IF S(I)>R(I) THEN 250
240     PRINT #2,K(I);SPC(5);D$(I);SPC(18-LEN(D$(I)));Q(I)
250 NEXT I
260 CLOSE 2
270 END
7800 REM SET UP OUTPUT DEVICE
7810 PRINT
7820 INPUT"OUTPUT TO SCREEN OR PRINTER S/P";B$
7830 IF B$="S" THEN A$="SCRN:"
7840 IF B$="P" THEN A$="LPT1:"
7850 IF B$<>"S" AND B$<>"P" THEN 7820
7860 RETURN
```

Table A19 Stock file search

```
10 REM INTERROGATE STOCK DATA FILE
20 SCREEN 0:CLS:PRINT
30 DIM K(20),D$(20),S(20),C(20),R(20),Q(20)
40 INPUT"NAME OF DATA FILE";FT$
50 OPEN FT$ FOR INPUT AS #1
60 GOSUB 7800
70 OPEN A$ FOR OUTPUT AS #2
80 FOR I=1 TO 20
90    INPUT #1,K(I),D$(I),S(I),C(I),R(I),Q(I)
100     IF K(I)=9999 THEN 120
110 NEXT I
120 CLOSE 1:BEEP:CLS:PRINT
130 PRINT "STOCK FILE SEARCH"
140 PRINT "------------------"
150 PRINT
160 INPUT "ENTER SEARCH WORD";X$
170 L=LEN(X$):E=0:F=0
180 U$="-----------------------------"
190 PRINT #2,U$
200 PRINT #2,TAB(1);"CODE";SPC(3);"DETAILS";
210 PRINT #2,SPC(6);"STOCK"
220 PRINT #2,U$
230 FOR I=1 TO 20
240    IF K(I)=9999 THEN 350
250    E=E+1:W=LEN(D$(I))-L+1
260    FOR J=1 TO W
270       Z$=MID$(D$(I),J,L)
280       IF Z$<>X$ THEN 330
290       F=F+1
300       PRINT #2,K(I);SPC(2);D$(I);
310       PRINT #2,SPC(13-LEN(D$(I)));S(I)
320       J=W
330    NEXT J
340 NEXT I
350 PRINT #2,U$
360 PRINT #2,E;"RECORDS READ"
370 PRINT #2,F;"RECORDS LISTED"
380 PRINT #2," ":PRINT #2," "
390 INPUT "ANOTHER SEARCH Y/N";A$
400 IF A$="Y" THEN 150
410 IF A$<>"N" THEN 390
420 CLOSE 2
430 END
7800 REM SET UP OUTPUT DEVICE
7810 PRINT
7820 INPUT"OUTPUT TO SCREEN OR PRINTER S/P";B$
7830 IF B$="S" THEN A$="SCRN:"
7840 IF B$="P" THEN A$="LPT1:"
7850 IF B$<>"S" AND B$<>"P" THEN 7820
7860 RETURN
```

Appendix B

Answers to Problems

Chapter 5

1 CALCULATIONS FOR DIFFERENT CODES

CODE	X	Y	CALC. VALUE
3	51	4	204
1	25	13	38
2	8	34	−26
5	4	3	64
4	62	5	12.4

Chapter 6

1 RADIUS = 443.334 M

2 VOLUME OF CUBOID = 155.8 CUBIC CM
VOLUME OF CYLINDER = 111.34 CUBIC CM
VOLUME OF HEXAGONAL BAR = 103118 CUBIC CM

Chapter 11

2 REAL ROOTS: −.24 AND −2.76
COMPLEX ROOTS
COINCIDENT ROOTS: 4
REAL ROOTS: .85 AND −2.35
REAL ROOTS: −1 AND   .33
COMPLEX ROOTS
COINCIDENT ROOTS: −.5

3 WIDTH OF SLIT = .0675 CM

4   Slope = 0.1096
Coefficient of correlation = 0.9953
Young's modulus = $1.92 \times 10^{11}\,\text{Nm}^{-2}$

5   The answer will vary slightly depending upon the selection of random numbers but should be close to 11.1 weeks.

6   Monthly repayments = 156.97 and 209.29, respectively.

Appendix C

ASCII Code (64 Character Set)

Character	Decimal Value	Character	Decimal Value
space	32	0	48
!	33	1	49
"	34	2	50
#	35	3	51
$	36	4	52
%	37	5	53
&	38	6	54
'	39	7	55
(	40	8	56
)	41	9	57
*	42	:	58
+	43	;	59
,	44	<	60
−	45	=	61
.	46	>	62
/	47	?	63

@	64	P	80
A	65	Q	81
B	66	R	82
C	67	S	83
D	68	T	84
E	69	U	85
F	70	V	86
G	71	W	87
H	72	X	88
I	73	Y	89
J	74	Z	90
K	75	[	91
L	76	\	92
M	77	]	93
N	78	^	94
O	79	_	95

Index

Index

ABS, 39
American Standard Code for
    Information Interchange
    (ASCII), 3, 48, 161
AND, 115
antilogarithms, *see* EXP
arctangent, *see* ATN
arguments, 38
    dummy, 46
arithmetic
    and logic unit, 1
    expressions, 15
    operations, 13
    operators, 15
arrays
    dimensioning, 73
    naming, 73
    subscripts, 73
ASC, 49
ASCII, 3, 48, 161
ATN, 43
AUTO, 10
average of three numbers
    flowchart, 25

backing storage devices, 1
BASIC, methods of translation,
    4
BEEP, 135
binary, 3
bit, 3
brackets, use of, 15

branch
    conditional, 29
    GOTO, 28
    IF . . . THEN, 29
    IF . . . THEN . . . ELSE, 29,
        32
    instruction, 28
    ON . . . GOSUB, 114
    ON . . . GOTO, 34
byte, 3

central processor, 1
character codes, 48
CHR$, 48
CIRCLE, 65
CLEAR, 27
clear screen, 11
CLOSE, 123
CLS, 11
codes, character, 48
colour, *see* COLOR
compiler, 4
conditional statements, 29, 32, 34
constant, 5
    numeric, 14
CONT, 11
CONTROL key, 10
control unit, 1
COS, 42
cosh, 44
cosine, 42–3
    evaluation of, 97, 154

CP/M, 116
CSRLIN, 140
cursor, 6

DATA statements, 6, 42
data
  files, 121
  INPUT statement, 7, 124
DEF FN, 46
DELETE, 6
DIM, 73
dimensioning arrays, 73
documentation, 27
DRAW, 68
dry run, 26
dummy
  arguments, 46
  record, 125
  value, example of, 30
duration, of note, 91

e, 44
ELSE, 29, 32
END, 6, 11
equal to, 30
ERASE, 74
error
  execution, 24
  logical, 26
  syntax, 23
evaluation, order of, 15
execution errors, 24
EXP, 44
exponent, 14
exponential series, 96
exponentiation, 15

FILES, 118
files
  add records routine, 136
  change records routine, 138
  data, 121, 128
  delete records routine, 140
  end of file record, 125
  input-output statements, 124
  loading routine, 134

OPEN and CLOSE, 123
  processing example, 128–47
  search records routine, 144
  sequential, 121
financial applications, 108
flowchart, 23
  average of three numbers,
    25
  dummy record, 126
  file processing and reporting,
    131
  loop control, 30
  sampling, 88
  sorting numbers, 77
  symbols, 24
FOR . . . NEXT
  example, 33
  loops, 32
  nested, 36, 75
FRE, 27
frequency, sound, 95
function keys, 12
functions
  of a computer, 1
  exponential, 44
  hyperbolic, 44
  library, 39
  logarithmic, 44
  string, 48
  TAB, 45
  trignometric, 42
  user-defined, 46

GOSUB, 79
GOTO, 28
greater than, 30

headings
  format and layout of, 22
  outputting, 7
high-level language, 3
histogram
  pastureland, 84, 152
hyperbolic functions, 44

IF . . . THEN, 29

IF . . . THEN . . . ELSE, 29
  nested, 32
INKEY$, 51
INPUT, 7, 124
input
  devices, 1
  statements, 5, 7, 124
INPUT$, 62
insert/delete keys, 6
instruction, 1
INT, 39
interpreter, 4

jump, *see* branch

KEY, 12
KEY LIST, 12
KEY OFF, 12
KEY ON, 12
KILL, 119

LEFT$, 49
legato, 91
LEN, 49
less than, 30
LET, 13
library functions, 39
LINE, 62
line numbers, 5
linear regression, 100
LINE INPUT, 9
LIST, 6
lists, 71
LLIST, 11
LOAD, 11, 118
loading programs, 11
LOCATE, 51, 140
LOG, 44
logarithms, *see* EXP, LOG
logical error, 26
logical operators, 115
loop
  count, 31, 32
  flowchart of, 30
  nested, 36, 75
LPRINT, 11, 116

LPRINT USING, 19
LPT:, 114

machine code, 3
macro
  drawing language, 68
  sound language, 90
MAXFILES, 123
memory, main, 1
menu, 112, 128
MERGE, 119
MID$, 49
Monte Carlo simulation, 103
MSDOS, 116
musical note values, 90

NAME, 119
name, variable, 5
NEW, 10
note values, 92
numbers, types of, 14

ON . . . GOSUB, 114
ON . . . GOTO, 34
OPEN, 115, 123
operations, hierarchy of, 15
operators,
  arithmetic, 15
  logical, 115
OR, 115
OUTPUT AS, 115, 123
output
  designing, 21
  devices, 1
  layout of, 21
  statements, 5, 115, 123

PAINT, 63
PALETTE, 59
pattern positions, 57
PCDOS, 116
peripheral devices, 1
pie chart
  example (colour), 66
PLAY, 90
playing tunes, 93

plotting routine, 80
POS, 140
PRINT, 5, 112, 124
PRINT USING, 19
printer
  listing programs, 11
  output to, 11, 19, 112
  types of, 111
program,
  development, 21
  editing, 6
  entering, 6
  listing, 7, 11
  loading, 11, 118
  renumbering lines, 12
  saving, 11, 118
  structure, example of, 129
  testing, 23
  trace, 26
programs
  clock for two players, 50
  coloured mosaics, 55
  coloured pie chart, 66
  cylindrical tank diameters, 41
  file processing and reporting
    example, 128–47
  foreground, screen and border
    colours, 54
  frequency
    grouping routine, 83
    table routine, 84
  Frere Jacques tune, 93
  heat of combustion, 97
  histogram routine, 83
  linear regression, 101
  mortgage calculation, 109
  name and address, 10, 112
  overlapping triangles, 62
  palette colours, 60
  plotting routine, 81
  printer control, 115
  print selected number, 71
  range of notes, 92
  ringing phone routine, 94
  rounding examples, 40, 46
  sampling routine, 87

simulation problem, 104
SOUND demonstration, 95
tempo routine, 92
to add N numbers, 31, 33
to calculate e, 96
to draw a house, 69
to draw and paint ellipses, 66
to illustrate
  FOR . . . NEXT, 34
  nested FOR loops, 76
  SGN and SQR, 41
to output a rectangle, 36
two-tone siren, 94

random numbers, *see* RND
READ, 5
records, file, 121
rectangles, using LINE function,
  64
regression, linear, 100
relational
  expression, 29
  operators, 30
REM, 10
RENUM, 12
reports
  reorder, 143
  search, 144
  valuation, 146
RESTORE, 42
RETURN, 79
  key, 6
RIGHT$, 49
RND, 45
roots of quadratic equations, 98
rounding, 40, 46
RUN, 7

sampling, 86
SAVE, 11, 118
SCREEN, 58
screen
  clear, 11
  colour, 59
  editor, 6
  modes, 58

palettes, 59
width, 58
SCRN, 114
secondary storage devices, 1
separators, 5
series, 96
SGN, 39
simulation, 103
SIN, 43
sine, 42–3
sinh, 44
sorting numbers, 76
SOUND, 95
sound
  duration of note, 91
  frequency, 95
  legato, 91
  playing tunes, 93
  staccato, 91
  tempo, 92
SPC, 114
SQR, 38, 41
square root function, *see* SQR
staccato, 91
statement
  conditional, 29, 32, 34
STEP, 33
STR$, 50
string
  comparison, 32
  constant, 8
  functions, 48
  variables, 8

subroutine, 23, 79, *see also*
  GOSUB
subscripts, 73
SWAP, 78
syntax errors, 23
SYSTEM, 120

TAB, 45
tables, 71
tabulation, 99
TAN, 42
tangent, 42
tanh, 44
tempo, 92
testing programs, 23
TIME$, 51
trignometric functions, 42
TROFF, 26
TRON, 26
truncation, 39
tunes, playing, 93

units of a computer, 1
user-defined functions, 46

VAL, 50
variables, 5
VDU, *see* visual display unit
visual display unit, 1

WIDTH, 58
wild cards, 117

COMPUTERS AND THEIR USE

L. .R. CARTER and E. HUZAN

An exceptionally clear introduction, for anyone wishing to acquire a basic understanding of computers and how to use them.

This book assumes no previous knowledge of computing, and focuses on the practical aspects of using computer facilities for a wide range of specific applications. The authors first describe the main types of hardware – the basic unit and peripherals – and how they can be linked. They then look at software, and explain the essentials of computer programming and communicating with computers, before going on to describe data processing and other computer applications in the office, in industry and at home. The implications of computers for the individual and for society as a whole are also considered.

The book will be particularly valuable to those thinking of acquiring a microcomputer for their particular use, whether in the office or at home.

TEACH YOURSELF BOOKS

COMPUTER GRAPHICS

JOHN LANSDOWN

This uniquely practical guide explains how to program useful and effective graphics on your own micro system.

Starting from basics, the author looks first at input and output peripheral devices and explains the procedures for producing rectilinear figures and curved lines, before going on to describe the use of colour, shading, highlighting and perspective. He then explains how to achieve transformations and simple animation effects, in both 2-D and 3-D graphics.

The procedures and subroutines are given in a pseudo-code which can easily be translated into any of the main programming languages. All the necessary mathematics is fully explained, and the book is illustrated throughout with computer-generated diagrams produced using the techniques described in the text.

This authoritative handbook provides a comprehensive introduction to graphics programming, with practical advice which will be invaluable to students and hobbyists alike.

TEACH YOURSELF BOOKS

THE POCKET CALCULATOR

L. R. CARTER and E. HUZAN

A practical handbook to help you master the techniques of using a pocket calculator.

This book explains calculator applications ranging from the basic arithmetical functions to a wide variety of mathematical, scientific, financial and statistical problems. As such, it is a book both for the beginner and for those wishing to make full use of the facilities available and get the most out of their calculator.

The techniques described are applicable to pocket and programmable calculators alike, and are fully illustrated with examples and exercises (with answers) at varying levels of difficulty.

TEACH YOURSELF BOOKS

COMPUTER PROGRAMMING IN PASCAL

DAVID LIGHTFOOT

Pascal is a general-purpose computer language which has become popular for its compact yet powerful facilities on a wide variety of microcomputers (including personal computers) and mainframe systems alike.

The simple nature of Pascal makes for clearly structured programming giving rise to programs which are easy to read, modify and show to be correct. As such, it is also one of the easier computer languages to learn.

This book provides a sound introduction to Pascal in its standard (BSI) and UCSD implementations. David Lightfoot first describes its general rules and standard types. Then, with the aid of many examples and illustrations, he gives a step-by-step explanation of Pascal statements and syntax – including branching, looping and dealing with sequential files – and practical advice on program design. Exercises (with answers) are included to give a thorough grounding in programming for a wide range of applications, while a graded selection of sample programs highlights the flexibility offered by Pascal.

TEACH YOURSELF BOOKS